THE ULTIMATE CHAUFFEUR

MASTERING THE ART OF PROFESSIONALISM FROM BEHIND THE WHEEL.

WRITTEN BY
ALISSON T. GUIMARAES

Title: The Ultimate Chauffeur:
The art of mastering professionalism from behind the wheel.

Author: Alisson T. Guimaraes
Book Cover by Emily Whiting
Editorial by Emily LeVault
Interior Design by HMDPUBLISHING
Pictures by Alisson T. Guimaraes
First edition 2024 © TXu002440863 / 2024-07-24

Paperback	ISBN # 979-8-9914077-0-0
Hardcover	ISBN # 979-8-9914077-1-7
E-Book	ISBN # 979-8-9914077-2-4
Audio Book	ISBN # 979-8-9914077-3-1

Executive Chauffeur course can be accessed at:

WWW.ULTIMATECHAUFFEUR.COM

"Never put off until tomorrow what you can do today"
Thomas Jefferson

CONTENTS

INTRODUCTION

Before we go into the extremely detailed functions of professionalism applied as an Executive Chauffeur, I will share with you an overview of my background, my journey to becoming an Executive Chauffeur, and the benefits of becoming an Executive Chauffeur.

The beginning of my story in America started with my father, who, during my early childhood, had left Brazil to seek a better life in the United States of America. He sacrificed a few years of his life by being apart from the family and living in the United States. After a few years, he went back to Brazil with high hopes of being successful, but he knew that he would be able to provide a better life for his family by being in the United States. He packed his bags once again and left Brazil. After one year of preparation, he was able to bring us, my mother, my brother and I, to live with him in the land of opportunities.

I arrived in the United States with my mother and my younger brother in the year 2000. We did not know how to communicate in English since we had only studied the language for a few weeks before we embarked on our journey to the land of the free and the home of the brave.

My family and I settled in the village of Port Chester in the state of New York, where I went to private school for the first year and then transferred to a public middle school. We had no means of communication, so we felt very lonely with no friends. It was a huge change from interacting with friends and family daily in Brazil to not communicating with them at all, because technology was not as advanced as it is today. Private school was especially hard because English was the only language spoken there, except for a few Hispanic children who spoke Spanish.

I did not realize that in my first year in America, I was learning and improving my English just by listening to it. I could not verbally respond to anyone in English, but I was listening and trying to use body language as a source of communication. It turned out that I was learning how to be a good listener and listening was an incredibly important skill to have, because it was the foundation of learning how to properly speak the language.

Once I moved into public school, I was surrounded by children and teachers from various Spanish-speaking countries who welcomed me and taught me how to speak Spanish. Since Spanish is one of the romance languages just like Portuguese is, I used the power of assimilation to figure out meanings and proper use of words. In turn, this process helped me communicate with people who could teach me proper English. After only four years of living in the United States, I had Portuguese as my first language, Spanish as my second language, and English as my third language.

I graduated from middle school in 2004 and moved onto high school where I started studying Italian as my fourth language. In high school I was exposed to many subjects that fueled my hunger for knowledge. The main subjects that kept my attention were math, science, language, and art. I also tried every sport that was available to me, but I was never the most athletic person.

In 2005, I got my first job at an Italian restaurant working as a busboy. That first job provided me the opportunity to earn some money, practice speaking Italian, learn accountability and learn people skills; all while attending school full time.

I graduated from high school in 2007 with high SAT scores and scholarships to three different colleges. I decided to go to Westchester Community College because I would save on the cost of my education and transfer after the two-year program. During those two years of Community College, I was still working in the restaurant business and found it hard to focus on school since all my friends and acquaintances kept exposing me to late parties and fun events. My grades were not the best, and I was only doing enough schoolwork to get a passing grade. I graduated from Westchester Community College with an associate's degree in arts and science with a focus on business, then transferred into the Hagan School of Business at IONA College.

During my time at IONA College, I was still working in restaurants, and I was still partying hard, but I was more focused on success. During that time, I was dating Monique, who is now my wife and is whom I have two beautiful daughters with, Elena and Rebecca. She was the one that put me back in a state of progress and values which were nonexistent for me during those rowdy times. She held me accountable for my actions, which helped me progress even more. I graduated in 2013 with a bachelor's degree and majored in international business administration.

I wanted to continue my formal education and complete an MBA. However, I was eager to go into the professional workforce and to be productive. Right after I graduated, I landed an incredible job providing financial services for car dealerships, where I learned many valuable lessons from my superiors. I was already great at dealing with people because of my many years working at restaurants, but that job taught me how to deal with high-net-worth individuals and people who are in positions of power. It also taught me about the financial side of the automobile industry.

Unfortunately, the company downsized because of legal troubles, and I was let go. I tried to stay in the industry, but the market was over-saturated and had huge barriers to entry. It got to the point where I was not learning anything and felt very unproductive.

From that point on, I jumped from job to job, trying to figure out where I really wanted to invest my time. I applied to many job positions online, I had nine interviews, and I was hired seven times. Unfortunately, all those job offers did not fulfill their promises. I ended up working in several jobs in the process of finding something fulfilling. From selling cable TV, to selling cell phone plans, to selling credit card processing, to selling cars, to selling H-VAC service contracts, to selling solar systems, to selling makeup door to door for a company that said I would be working on a marketing project for a sports team; absolutely all of these jobs did not have "selling" on the job description. The job search was ruthless!

I felt discouraged from all the "bait and switching" that I had experienced on these online job offers. One night while talking to a friend, I was suggested to drive for a limousine company while I figured out what I really wanted to do. I was skeptical, but I entertained the idea since it would be a good opportunity to get away from sales. I would also have a flexible schedule so that I could work on my next professional career move.

I was always a great driver, so this job was supposed to be easy. I got a taxi and livery service license from New York and applied to the first limousine company that I found on the internet. Their office was surprisingly close to my home, which made it convenient. I went through the interview process and started on the job the very next day.

I have always been very particular about cleanliness and organization, so my priority was to work in a clean and organized vehicle. I would always arrive early to make sure that I had a clean vehicle to work with. Every day I drove a different vehicle, so the cleaning chores became a routine and I quickly learned that different people have different tolerance levels for cleanliness and hygiene.

I also started observing other Chauffeurs to see how I could improve on the job. Through these observations, I realized that there are too many unqualified individuals working in this industry. Once I noticed that pattern, I started taking notes on everything that I thought could be improved on. And that was the beginning of my journey to becoming an Executive Chauffeur.

This journey has made me identify many benefits of providing transportation that are overlooked by most people, both who provide transportation services and those who use transportation services.

The first and obvious benefit of being a Chauffeur is that a Chauffeur will travel and experience many places, since every passenger is picked up at a different location and dropped off at different destinations. At these places, a Chauffeur will experience different local streets, different cities, different states, and sometimes different countries. Not only that, but when a Chauffeur is at those places, he/she will experience different architecture, different engineering, different art pieces, different tourist attractions, different scenery, to name a few. While traveling to all different places, Chauffeurs could also experience many cultural events, music, foods, and drinks.

Now that we have identified the geographical benefits, we can address the human experience and, by human experience, I mean every interaction with a person. If we observe closely, everyone has a different story to tell, since they are all different. Chauffeurs are exposed to different personalities, gender, race, age, place of origin, culture, language, financial status, social status, job titles, job descriptions, interests, needs and many more attributes that make every individual unique.

Fortunately, most people enjoy a good conversation and are willing to share experiences and knowledge. This fact makes the job of a Chauffeur an incredible source of knowledge and opportunities. Essentially transforming the job of a Chauffeur from transporting a passenger from point A to point B to profiting and expanding knowledge at the same time.

While being a Chauffeur, you will learn with every interaction, and here is why. Whenever a Chauffeur drives for a lawyer, he/ she will learn the language of law and its industry or specifics of the job. If the Chauffeur drives for a brain surgeon, he/she will learn the medical language and its industry or specifics of the job. This concept applies to every professional with different job titles that a Chauffeur is exposed to. Other examples would be driving for singers, actors and actresses, comedians, politicians, doctors, priests, restaurateurs, investors, managers, models, CEO's, CFO's, CMO's, CIO's, scientists, inventors, writers and the list goes on and on.

Building meaningful relationships that generate revenue is another benefit of being a Chauffeur. A client that appreciates a Chauffeur's service can request that specific Chauffeur every time they use the service. As the relationship grows between the Chauffeur and the client, the Chauffeur will have the opportunity to ask for referrals and online reviews. When this happens, the Chauffeur will gain control over their schedule and their income will increase. Gaining control of the schedule means that the Chauffeur will have first choice on the jobs that he/she wants to work based on monetary value, time, or benefits. Additionally, he/she will increase their income because he/she will have more work available to them and their commissions will increase as he/she provides more value.

This process of meeting new clients, gaining their trust by providing superior service and asking for request and referrals is repeated over and over with every client. Therefore, building great relationships with everyone you meet can lead to positive financial outcomes and a better use of time.

Now that you know a little about my story, how I became an Executive Chauffeur and the benefits of being a Chauffeur, I will share all the information that I have learned throughout my years as an Executive Chauffeur. The information in this book is presented in such a format that is easy for you to go back to it for a reference at any moment. So, make sure to carry this book with you as a guide to successfully servicing a client.

OVERVIEW

In order for a Chauffeuring business to be successful and generate revenue, that business needs to fully understand their customers wants and needs. Only after they have mastered this important skill that the business can start charging to fulfill those wants and needs. The information in this book shows you exactly what a paying customer wants and expects from a Chauffeured service. It is up to you to make it a reality for those paying customers!

DEFINITION

A Chauffeur is defined in the dictionary as a person employed to drive a private or rented automobile for a certain amount of time to and from certain destinations. However, a Chauffeur is much more than that!

A true Chauffeur will be described in its entirety in this book. At the end, you will understand that every part of this training is important, and you will be equipped with all the information necessary to become part of the best in the industry!

IMPRESSIONS

The word "impression" is defined as an idea, feeling, or opinion about something or someone, especially one formed without conscious thought or on the basis of little evidence.

First Impressions

First impressions are all about the first few seconds of when you meet somebody. Unknowingly, you judge others and others judge you. This is only nature playing its part and more often than not, it cannot be controlled. First impressions are so important because they dictate the outcome of a relationship, either personal or professional. You must be aware that you are always being judged so that you can work on how your image is perceived by others.

The first impressions of a Chauffeur start with the communication language used when reaching out to the client. Does the Chauffeur use properly formed sentences with proper punctuation? (Ex: Hello Mr. Smith, I am Executive Chauffeur Alisson. I'm ready at your convenience.) Or does the Chauffeur use common language that he/she uses amongst friends and family? (Ex: Hey John, let's hit the road cause there is a lot of traffic and I gotta make my next pickup.)

The next step to first impression judgement is how the Chauffeur arrives driving the vehicle and how the vehicle is presented. Does the Chauffeur arrive in a timely fashion with a crisp, clean vehicle? (Ex: Arrive fifteen minutes early with a vehicle that looks like it just got out of the showroom.) Does the Chauffeur park the vehicle in a safe and well-presented place with easy access to entering and exiting the vehicle? (Ex: Drive the vehicle as if you are showing it off and park with the vehicle's door in direct line of access with no obstructions such as potholes, steps, garbage cans, trees, etc., whenever possible.)

The next step to first impression judgement is when the Chauffeur gets out of the vehicle. Does the Chauffeur get out of the car with class, or do they struggle because they are overweight, or is it the way they parked the car? While all this is happening, your client is also looking at your attire, facial expressions and what you sound like. (Ex: Dress in a proper suit, smile, and talk in a formal manner.) All these aspects of first impressions are very important because they are irreversible; so, you must get it right the first time or it can cost you the desired outcome.

Visual Positive First Impression

Here is an example of how a visual positive first impression provided me with an opportunity for repeat business. I was dispatched along with three other Chauffeurs to service a new client who was flying into a luxury FBO in a private airport in NY. The main client, who is the owner of a multi-billion-dollar company, was accompanied by three of his Executives and their assistants. Our job was to transport each one of them and their assistant to a few corporate meetings in New York City, then to a well-known Steak House for dinner and back to the private airport where their corporate jet was waiting to take them back to where they came from.

When I was first notified of the job, I immediately went over all the information with dispatch and made sure to have as much client contact information as possible. Initially, I only had one phone number to use, but after a few minutes of persuasion, I was provided with the phone numbers of all four assistants. I got the luxury SUV ready by making it look as if it had just come out of the showroom and started doing research on every passenger on the list. I found out who was the main client by researching on the internet and I also found information on what he likes by looking at his social media. I added his favorite candy and beverage in the vehicle and did the same with his assistant. After I had the vehicle prepared, I headed to the private airport and went inside the FBO to check in before any of the other Chauffeurs arrived.

When the other Chauffeurs arrived, I took notice that all three vehicles were dirty on the outside and, as each Chauffeur exited their vehicles, I felt more and more convinced that there would be a preference to ride with me as the Chauffeur. One of the Chauffeurs was wearing a light grey suit with a pink shirt and red tie, the second Chauffeur was wearing a proper Chauffeur uniform but was not wearing a tie and the third Chauffeur was wearing a wrinkled white shirt that was not fully tucked into his pants, black dress pants and a black tie but no suit jacket. I was wearing a full Chauffeur suit with a dark color tie and shined shoes.

After talking to the other Chauffeurs and identifying their strengths and weaknesses, I sent a greeting message to all the assistants telling them that I was ready at their convenience and that it would take a certain amount of time to reach their first destination. We were called by the FBO to follow an airport personnel into the tarmac and stage the vehicles. I made sure to go in first and picked the spot closest to the red carpet that was rolled out, waiting for the plane to park. I stayed outside the vehicle, standing by the passenger door, awaiting the clients to deplane as all other Chauffeurs stayed inside their vehicles. Just as I had planned, they all flocked towards me. (The one who imposed the best first impression).

I ended up driving for the main client and by making sure that I would be driving for him; I gave myself the opportunity to provide a unique experience that led to repeat requests by him and his assistant.

Right Type of First Impression

The next example will show how important it is to impose the right type of first impression. I received the job one day in advance, so I had plenty of time to prepare for it. On that specific service, two Chauffeurs were to arrive at a FBO in a private airport in Long Island, NY, at 9:45 a.m.. Pick up a famous actress and her large amount of luggage and drop her off at her luxurious apartment in New York City. Now, this sounds like a very simple job for most people, but great opportunities only appear to those who can create them.

As per usual, I researched the client online and gathered as much information as I could about her likes and dislikes. I found out that she loves Ghirardelli Sea Salt Chocolate, Sparkling water and enjoys listening to classical music. Furthermore, I was able to learn about where she has traveled to, what kind of activities she enjoys and her political values. All this information made me prepared to engage in conversation if she was willing to converse. The information prepared me so that I knew how to dialogue without saying things that would not please her, would not create discomfort or create unwanted disagreements.

I was very surprised when I arrived at the airport twenty minutes early. I was surprised because the other Chauffeur was already there with the same type of vehicle as I was driving and it was spotless, just like my vehicle. As the other Chauffeur got out of his vehicle to come greet me, I was even more surprised; we were about the same age, same stature and had the same attitude. But there was one thing that he did wrong. He did not look like a Chauffeur. He was wearing a freshly pressed Armani brown suit, a white Luis Vuitton button-down shirt with two open buttons, a Gucci Belt with a quite bright buckle, and Ferragamo's shoes with no socks.

To tell you the truth, I thought that he was going to win this client over me, but boy was I wrong. We went inside the FBO to check in and while he went to the bathroom, I picked a couple of high-end magazines to put in the car for the client. I sent a customized text message to the client's assistant and waited for instructions from the airport personnel. We headed back to our vehicles and waited for almost two hours until the plane landed, and we were clear to go onto the tarmac.

As we staged the vehicles, I felt a little intimidated by how good the other Chauffeur looked and the only thing that went through my mind was that I was going to be stuck carrying luggage. We both parked our vehicles in a very presentable fashion and we both stood outside by the passenger's door waiting to greet this famous actress. But, a few minutes later, the other Chauffeurs posture changed. He was very relaxed, leaned against the vehicle, crossed his legs, dropped his Ray Bans to the tip of his nose and put his hands in his pocket. At that point, he did not play the part of a Chauffeur anymore. He looked as if he was a very wealthy guy waiting to get on the chartered plane when it was clear.

The private jet landed, and the actress came out asking if I was Chauffeur Alisson and at that point my mindset changed and I was back in the game. I had won the challenge of who was going to drive for the famous actress. After she got settled in the car, she said, "I wonder who is the fancy guy that is waiting to use the jet?" I laughed and replied to her: "He is not here to use a jet; he is the one that will take all of your luggage to your apartment." Then she affirmed: "He certainly doesn't look like he would be doing that kind of work and I would be very confused if he was the one driving for me." I gave the guy credit for trying to give a good first impression and changed the subject.

Proactive First Impression

The next example shows how a great proactive first impression served in my favor when I was dispatched to pick up a high-profile client at a red-carpet event in New York City. I received the job from the dispatching office and as per usual I went over all the information provided. I did the necessary research on the passenger and got to work adding custom treats, some energy drinks, and The New York Times newspaper to the vehicle. There was one thing that was different this time. I was assigned a pristine Black on Black 2002 Lincoln Town Car with approximately 230,000 miles on the odometer.

When I arrived at the event, I parked in the back of the building as instructed. There were also three other very expensive and new luxury vehicles on location with Chauffeurs. I always talk to other Chauffeurs when I have the chance because I can always learn something from other's experiences. So, I asked what company they worked for? how long they have been working as Chauffeurs? And who they were going to service that night?

I was incredibly surprised to hear that there were four different companies on location to service the same passenger. Naturally, I measured up my competition, identified their strengths and weaknesses and started being proactive because I knew that I didn't have much of a chance at winning when given the choice between the vehicles. I called dispatch to explain the situation and to make sure that we had as much information as possible on the passenger. I talked to security and gained information on where the passenger would come through and the time it would take for him to get to the vehicles after his performance.

With all the information I had, I repositioned my vehicle to be in direct access to the passenger, while blocking the view to the other vehicles. My next move was to get the other Chauffeurs distracted by making them talk to each other. My plan worked like a charm! I timed the passenger's arrival to the location and stood right next to the passenger's door. I texted all parties involved. I informed them of my location and gave them a detailed description of who and what to look for when outside.

The passenger came out of the venue with security and came directly into my vehicle without any hesitation. I introduced myself and his immediate comment was that he was not expecting to be riding in a classic and that he is usually riding in brand new vehicles. My response to him was that he should enjoy the ride, because he would probably not have the chance to ride that type of vehicle for too many more times as the vehicle was only used occasionally unless specifically requested and approved by the owner.

In these three instances, you can see how much the theme of first impressions is complex. The first example illustrated how a great visual first impression is important. The second example shows how sometimes your imposed first impressions can propose or give the illusion of you being someone or something that you are not. The third example shows how being proactive and setting expectations can impose a great first impression and make others go un-noticed. You must also take notice that there is one thing that all these examples have in common, which is proper communication with the clients and passengers.

Never forget that you are a Chauffeur, and you need to look like and act like a Chauffeur in order to succeed.

Now that first impressions are out of the way; you need to focus on maximizing positive current impressions that will lead to positive lasting impressions. All sections of this book are designed to help you impose the best first impressions and maximize positive lasting impressions on the ones you are meeting for the first time and/or to your repeat passengers.

2

MINDSET

By acknowledging that becoming an Executive Chauffeur will take time and intentional effort, you must maintain a positive mindset. The following information can be used to develop a plan of action so that you can enjoy the journey of becoming a successful Executive Chauffeur. This will hopefully lead you toward a healthier and more rewarding work environment where personal growth can be achieved in an accelerated way.

Professional Mindset

The professional mindset of a Chauffeur means that they apply the following:

- **E**xecutive Chauffeurs have a Can-do attitude and will not stop until they are able to satisfy their customers wants and needs.

Satisfying your customer's wants and needs can be incredibly challenging, but there are a few ways to make that task easier. The first step is to research your client or passenger on the internet. Learn everything possible about your clients or passengers. Research personality, culture, place of origin, religion, political views, medical conditions, place of work, economic status, preferred foods and beverages, favorite sports, favorite TV shows, movies, music, etc. The second step is to set expectations. You can start setting expectations on your first contact with your client and that can be through text message, a phone call, or in person. Inform your client or passenger of who you are, where you are, how long it will take for them to arrive at their destination, any foreseeable traffic conditions, weather conditions etc.... The third step is to have all appropriate amenities in the vehicle, such as, phone chargers, tissues, water, hand sanitizer, napkins, note pads, newspapers, etc.... The fourth step is making a strong effort to satisfy spontaneous requests such as arriving at their destination at a specific time, making unexpected stops along the ride, complete given tasks while the passenger or client is away from the vehicle.

- **E**xecutive Chauffeurs always try to be the best with a healthy competitiveness, which means Executive Chauffeurs want to be better than the competition.

Competition is in human nature, and it is necessary to create success stories. One way that you can become better than the competition is by having the mentality of constant learning because the more you know, the better off you are. A second way of being better than the competition is to be proactive in sales, to identify opportunities to pitch and to naturally encourage repeat business and referrals. A third way of being better that the competition is to be proactive in thinking ahead of the competition or to be better prepared than the competition. There are many ways in which you can be better than the competition and it is up to you to identify how you can play your strengths against your competitor's weaknesses.

- **E**xecutive Chauffeurs are meticulous with process and cleanliness, which means they have a process to follow and they must pay very close attention to details.

Every Executive Chauffeur is detail-oriented and strives for perfection. One way to make the job a little easier is to have a step-by-step process on everything that involves servicing a client. For example, a process could be learning about your upcoming jobs, getting prepared to service that specific client, cleaning the vehicle on the inside by blowing air into crevices, using a microfiber cloth to dust the interior and eliminate handprints, adding the amenities, etc.... The process needs to be whatever works for you, but it must be optimized for efficiency.

- **E**xecutive Chauffeurs practice until it becomes second nature, which means they want to be proficient at the job.

Becoming proficient at the job is incredibly challenging and takes time. It involves taking the job very seriously and attacking the very steep learning curve that takes you from one phase to the next. When a Chauffeur becomes an Executive Chauffeur, it means that he or she went through all the phases in the career. Driver, Chauffeur, Senior Chauffeur and Executive Chauffeur. Proficiency happens in the Senior Chauffeur phase, and it generally involves having knowledge of and having the ability to apply; route management, time management, communication skills, and optimized process to the daily jobs. You can only be considered an Executive Chauffeur after you become proficient as a Senior Chauffeur and start taking initiative toward adding value and increasing customer base and customer retention.

- **E**xecutive Chauffeurs take and accept responsibility, which means they are willing to learn from problems and mistakes.

Executive Chauffeurs view every negative situation as an opportunity to learn and, by taking ownership of the situation, they are more likely to become problem solvers. Hurdles can appear at any moment, so it is especially important for Executive Chauffeurs to de-escalate situations and provide solutions. Here is an example of how accepting responsibility has made me a problem solver for one client. I was servicing a multibillionaire client in New York City on a Friday afternoon. Traffic was accumulating during rush hour, and I was to take the client to JFK Airport for a 7:15 p.m. flight. I had warned the client about growing traffic during rush hour on Fridays, but the client was still late to begin our trip to the airport. Since clients are always right, even when they are not, I worried I might be blamed for a missed flight. So, I started to plan. The client came to the vehicle and demanded to be on time for the flight. I responded, you will only be on time if you trust me with a new plan because if we continue with the original plan, you will be 45 minutes late. The client agreed by saying, "Whatever it takes, just get me there!" I immediately called the client's assistant and told her to charter a helicopter departing from the east side heliport ASAP to fly the client to a private FBO at JFK. I also booked an affiliate Chauffeur to take the client from the FBO to the commercial terminal. The client praised my efforts and showed much appreciation by giving a generous monetary bonus and requesting me as their preferred service provider. Taking and accepting responsibility is extremely important for personal growth and it often requires preemptive thinking.

Body & Mind

Executive Chauffeurs will always be worried about their body and their mind as it is the foundation for a healthy lifestyle and professional appearance. This means they

- Shower every day before going to work.
- Shave or trim their body hair and/or facial hair.
- Maintain a discrete haircut.
- Use odorless deodorant and/or mild perfume or cologne to manage body odor.
- Brush and floss their teeth. A beautiful smile is essential for first impressions!
- Eat healthy. The body needs the energy to endure the long hours ahead.
- Exercise. Executive Chauffeurs must be in shape in order to execute the job and project a healthy appearance at all times.
- Get enough sleep!
- Reserve time to spend with themselves. A healthy mind is essential to keep up with the daily activities.

Sleep

Get enough sleep! Working in the transportation industry can be very demanding of your time and too often drivers get caught doing time extensive jobs during times where their body should be resting in the form of sleep.

Getting enough sleep has three major benefits which are It increases your concentration levels, which allows you to learn new things faster and maintain focus of specific tasks. It boosts your immune system so you can avoid getting sick or if you do get sick, you can recover faster. Lastly, getting enough sleep naturally improves your emotional well-being.

During sleep, human growth hormone is released from your brain, it helps your body grow, repair any damages, and build muscle.

The most important role of sleep is its role in learning and memory!

Memory formation is broken down into three processes, the first is encoding, which happens when you are awake and take in new information. The second is consolidation, this happens when you sleep, and the new information is stored in your brain. The third is retrieval, which is when stored information in your brain is accessed and recalled or when you remember information.

If you are in a situation where you need to stay awake while you should be sleeping, make sure that you have enough energy to stay awake.

- Munch on high energy foods such as trail mix or chew gum so that your brain is focused on a task and your body can stay awake.
- Talking to someone keeps your mind busy and engaged, so it will also help you stay awake, especially if the conversation is engaging.
- Listen to podcasts that activate your curiosity and engage your intellect because it keeps your brain working and focused on something other than sleep.
- Take a fifteen to twenty minute nap if you don't have any passengers or clients on board your vehicle. Naps will help you restore energy and help you stay awake.
- Drink coffee or high caffeine drinks, so you will get a boost of energy that will also help you stay awake.
- Lastly, you should frequently get out of your vehicle and walk somewhere that has bright lights and people walking around. Getting your blood flowing by walking or exercising and engaging your brain in activities will help you stay awake for longer periods of time.

As you can observe, taking care of your body is extremely important because it is the basis of body and mind health. When you take good care of your body, you are more likely to have high self-esteem and be more motivated. A high self-esteem makes you feel positive about yourself, positive about your actions and positive about your future. High self-esteem will also leave you feeling motivated and restless to achieve any goal. So, take good care of your body and your mind!

Source: https://bokcenter.harvard.edu/how-memory-works#:~:text=There%20are%20three%20main%20processes,Encoding.

Behavior

Behavior is defined in the dictionary as the way in which one acts or conducts oneself, especially toward others. With that being said, there is nothing more attractive than a person that exudes confidence, structure, and trust through their behavior. The following are behaviors that can make a person more professionally attractive.

- Always have a proper introduction when meeting someone.
- Firm handshake and eye contact when appropriate.
- Stand tall and confident so the client feels safe.
- Keep your hands out of your pockets.
- Get rid of bad habits (No Smoking, no chewing gum, biting nails, etc.)
- Restrict yourself from making noise, tapping, singing, humming, scratching, blowing your nose loudly, coughing, picking your nose when clients are in the car.
- Be polite and filter your words. (Do not swear!)
- Be silent and do not force conversation.
- Act intelligent and be able to carry a conversation when appropriate.

Invest in Yourself

Investing in yourself can be challenging and overwhelming, since there are too many topics to learn. Here are 5 complex subjects that I have studied in a course called "Re-Learning Creativity", lectured by Murilo Gun. I personally think that these five subjects will make you a more successful Chauffeur because these concepts trigger a broader view of every day nuances, people, and situations.

1. Intrapersonal Intelligence. The capacity or ability to connect with yourself, generate emotions, self-knowledge, and control fear.
2. Interpersonal Intelligence. The capacity or ability to create relationships, comprehend dreams and wishes or wants and needs, dialogue, and communicate thoughts and emotions.
3. Creative Intelligence. The capacity to approach new things, think outside the box, break standards or barriers, and innovate.
4. Inter-artificial Intelligence. The capacity to connect with technology, use and not be used by it, and take advantage of its potential.
5. Coachable Intelligence. The capacity to learn how to learn, change and adapt as things change, take responsibility, and enjoy learning.

Source: www.murilogun.com.br/cursos , Course Name: Reaprendizagem Criativa, Author: Murilo Gun

A busy mind is a healthy mind, so invest in yourself.

- Read books, newspapers, magazines etc. (get involved)
- Watch informative videos.
- Listen to podcasts.
- Research specific subjects or topics.
- Network.
- Build personal projects.
- Take courses.
- Improve your communication skills.
- Improve your qualifications.

Applied Knowledge is power!

The more you apply what you learn, the better off you will be.

3

APPEARANCE

Always remember that the first few seconds will dictate the rest!

A Chauffeur's uniform is more than just something to wear. It is a symbol of professionalism! The uniform sets Chauffeurs apart from other transportation professionals. It signals and supports their dedication to luxurious customer service. When Chauffeurs present themselves with crisp, clean uniforms, it makes all the difference in the world to clients who demand the best quality service.

What Kind of Shirt?

It is best for Chauffeurs to wear plain, collared, white dress shirts. Some companies may specify other acceptable colors, but, more often than not, a Chauffeur should wear white. This color allows Chauffeurs to maintain a certain level of style and class without drawing attention to themselves. As service-oriented professionals, it is important for Chauffeurs to be presentable and discreet.

Complete Suit

Chauffeurs should wear matching black or dark-colored suit jackets and suit pants. Jackets and pants should be simple: no unusual piping, decorations, or designs. The Chauffeur's suit should not call attention to him or her; rather it should help the Chauffeur stay discrete. Have your suit freshly dry-cleaned and pressed on a regular basis. Chauffeurs should always wear a suit jacket even in warm weather.

Socks and Shoes

A Chauffeur's feet should match their suit—black dress socks and shined black dress shoes are essential. No visible logos or designs. High-quality leather shoes can be easily cleaned and shined every day. Do not use overly shiny shoes as it attracts too much attention to your feet.

Accessories

Depending on the weather, a company's specific dress code, or the type of client a Chauffeur services, Chauffeurs may also need the following accessories:

Overcoats

In cold weather, Chauffeurs may wear plain overcoats that match the color of their suits. Whenever a Chauffeur does wear an overcoat, they should be sure to wear a suit jacket under their coat. Chauffeurs should never wear overcoats over collared shirts without a suit jacket.

Ties

Chauffeurs should wear black or discreet ties. Tie clips are optional. Some companies may have specific ties that feature a company logo. They should always wear The Full Windsor Knot! As it represents power and structure. Your tie's height should be right above the belt Line and at most one finger width above the belt line.

Belts

As the old etiquette dictates, a Chauffeur's belt should match their shoes. Therefore, Chauffeurs should wear black belts made of high-quality leather, with no logos, designs, or overly ornate buckles.

Gloves

Some companies require that Chauffeurs wear driving gloves. Gloves are usually plain black leather or plain white cotton, depending on the company's regulations.

Hats

Some companies also require that Chauffeurs wear plain black driving caps.

Jewelry

It is acceptable to wear subtle jewelry—wedding rings and chain necklaces worn under the shirt are two examples of jewelry that is permissible. However, too much "bling" looks very unprofessional. Always wear a discreet yet empowering watch in case your client asks for the time.

JOB SUCCESS

Your job success will depend on how you define your long-term goals so that you can properly apply the skill needed to accomplish your short-term or specific job goals through investing in yourself so that you can become a sought-after professional.

Career Goal

The ultimate career goal is to become an Executive Chauffeur and to do so you must go through all the phases necessary. The first phase is the DRIVER phase. The Driver phase is essentially everyone who has a valid driver's license and works in the transportation industry. The Driver phase requires very minimal communication skills and formality. The second phase is the CHAUFFEUR phase. The Chauffeur phase is one step above in the sense of formality. It means that the Driver now operates a luxury vehicle, wears a formal Chauffeur uniform and is in the process of learning the customer service aspect of the job and other skills. The third phase is the SENIOR CHAUFFEUR phase. The Senior Chauffeur phase is when the Chauffeur is in an advanced state of knowledge of what the job entails. The Senior Chauffeur takes their job seriously and cares about the customers experience, therefore, becoming a more reliable asset to any company or client. The final phase is the EXECUTIVE CHAUFFEUR phase. The Executive Chauffeur phase is when the Senior Chauffeur has mastered all attributes of customer service and elevates their worth within the business by becoming a reliable source of new revenue and by calling others to action so that you can scale positive outcomes.

Specific Job Goal

The specific goal of an Executive Chauffeur is to create and deliver a positive transportation and customer service experience that will make a positive impression that will last for years on your clients. By providing an extraordinary service with unparalleled luxury, an Executive Chauffeur will also create repeat business, service requests and new customer referrals that generate profit. However, taking the Executive Chauffeur job as a career involves much more than just increasing business.

The specific job goal of a professional Chauffeur is to:

- Provide a safe environment in the vehicle for passengers to be in.
- Pick up the client at the right location and at the right time.
- Deal with any luggage along with the client so that they know that their luggage is safe. If the client is of high profile, make sure the client is always safe while dealing with the luggage.
- Have the right amenities in the vehicle? (The difference between a limousine service and a taxi is YOU the Chauffeur!)
- Always maintain a pleasant environment inside the vehicle.
- Fulfill any requests your client/passenger might have.
- Provide a super smooth ride with precision and speed.

- Maintain proper communication with all parties involved.
- Deliver the client at the right location.
- Ask for requests and referrals.
- Sell and up sell at the right moment.
- Make sure they do not leave any belongings in the vehicle.
- Always protect the client's privacy.

Adding Value

Being an Executive Chauffeur is all about adding value. Adding value to yourself is the most important part of the career. There are many ways to add value to yourself, and here are some examples:

Obtain different operating licenses or permits that allow you to operate larger vehicles. This opens up more opportunities because you are increasing your exposure to a greater number of clients or passengers.

Create a list of written testimonials from your clients and passengers. Having a list of testimonials is an incredible way to market yourself.

Remain in a constant learning mode, absorbing as much useful information as possible. Learn about different cultures, languages, medicine, technology, politics, math, science, etc.... but the best subject to study is communication since it is one of the subjects that can accelerate your path to financial success.

Acquire a license to carry a firearm. Having a license to carry a firearm will make others view you as a protective person, therefore making customers feel safer around you and maybe pay extra to have you around as a source of protection. Some may be against having a license to carry but it is still important to go through training, especially if you carry a firearm and support the 2nd amendment.

Last, but not least, get a CPR certification. By getting CPR certified you will automatically attract clients who are more caring of their own lives and it will create a demand for your services. Consequently, your clients will believe that if their health is compromised during their trip, they will have a bigger chance of survival if they are being serviced by you.

Therefore, becoming an Executive Chauffeur is a long-term self-improvement project that will make you a more well-rounded individual with very desirable capabilities.

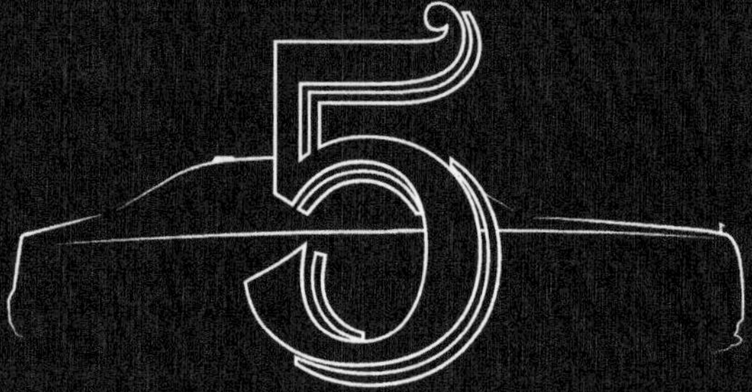

TIME MANAGEMENT

Time management is the process of planning and controlling how much time to spend on specific activities. Good time management enables an individual to complete more in a shorter period of time, lowers stress, and leads to career success.

"Time is free, but it is priceless. You cannot own it, but you can use it. You cannot keep it, but you can spend it. Once you have lost it, you can never get it back."

Harvey Mackay

- BE ON TIME for yourself
- BE ON TIME for your loved ones
- BE ON TIME for your boss
- BE ON TIME for your coworkers
- BE ON TIME for your client

Here are some reasons why you should never be late.

If you are late for yourself, your anxiety levels rise and you are more prone to make bad decisions like speeding and breaking the law to catch up on time. If you are late for your loved ones, they will feel like they are not important enough for your time and will build disappointment as they can't rely on you. If you are late for your boss, you will be considered unreliable and it will not be long until you lose your job. If you are late for your coworkers, you will be considered a drag because they will have to pick up your slack. If you are late for your client, you will certainly receive negative feedback and you will lose the client at some point. This will affect you because your reputation in the market place will be negative, your loved ones will look at you as a disappointment, your boss will be making notes on the negative consequences of you being late, and your coworkers will be out of work since you caused the client to replace service.

If you are ten minutes early, you are late! Always arrive at least 15 minutes early in case your client wants to leave early.

Never honk your horn when you arrive. Clients know that you are there because they hired your services and expect you to be on time.

Only knock on the door or ring the bell if your client does not respond to your text or call upon, your arrival.

6

COMMUNICATION

Communication is the most powerful weapon a man has! It is extremely important that you can communicate properly with everyone involved in the completion of the specific job. Proper communication is essential because it can mean a positive or a negative outcome to whatever you are doing.

- **V**erbal communication encompasses both how you deliver a message and how you receive it. People who can convey information clearly and effectively are highly valued by others.

- **N**onverbal communication is the communication between people through sending and receiving wordless clues. Body language, appearance, environment, tone of voice and touch are all nonverbal cues.

- **M**aintain clear and efficient communication with dispatch but keep it to a minimum.

- **W**hen executing a job, greet your clients properly, offer amenities, and engage in conversation if clients are willing to converse. Close to the end of the ride ask for referrals and do a proper farewell.

- **K**eep all information that you hear in the car to yourself. Clients expect the highest level of privacy and that you are professional enough to not share any information of what is done or said in the car.

Communication at its Finest

If a conversation arises with your client, follow these ten tips that are sourced from an article named 10 Tips to Talk About Anything with Anyone written by Dr. Susan Krauss Whitbourne:

1. Listen. You have two ears and one mouth so that you can listen more and talk less. Use it to your advantage, better listeners have better conversations.
2. Use reflecting skills. Repeat or reaffirm what you heard, or at least what you think you heard. This skill shows that you have been paying attention to what is being said. This skill also helps set a deeper position of your opinion or thoughts in the conversation.
3. Learn to read nonverbal cues. If the person seems uncomfortable with where the conversation is heading, shift gears. Though some people enjoy debating politics, religion, and sex, other people would rather keep things light. Learn how to gauge the impact of what you are saying by reading nonverbal cues such as posture, eye contact, and hand movements.
4. Avoid judging and coming to conclusions too early. If you follow the first three steps, you will be less likely to misinterpret the person you're talking to. Things are not always what they seem to be when talking to someone through a rear-view mirror so, it is important to interpret that person correctly.
5. Be a detective. Search the person online before meeting him or her. Look for occupation, education, common interest, etc. This will certainly help you create common ground with the individual and give relevance to the conversation.

6. Never assume that you share ideologies and opinions because you might be very wrong and create undesired debates or even come to confrontation. Opposite opinions make healthy conversation if you are open to accepting the other's opinion.
7. Try to learn from each interaction with a new person. A person you have never met before may have been places and done things that you have not done yet or will never do. People from other places, including countries other than your own, can give you new perspectives. They will only open up if you show that you are interested. People love talking about themselves. You can expand your knowledge of other regions, cultures, and nations, ultimately making you a more interesting conversationalist as well.
8. Being familiar with current events is absolutely the best way to have enough topics to bring up in any conversation. The topics do not have to involve in-depth knowledge, any up-to-date information is better than being oblivious to everything around you.
9. Know when not to talk. Some people prefer no conversation at all or are too busy to talk, especially in confined situations, such as private transportation. You might think it is great to spend the driving time in polite small talk, but the other person may not think the same. Most times, if you try to start a conversation with the passenger and their answers are short, such as yes or no, it most likely means that person does not want to engage in conversation for the duration.
10. Don't over-share. It is very common to get into subjects that make you want to share your experiences, but keep yourself in check. You never know what that person can do with the over shared information

and how they can use it against you or someone in common in the future. Over sharing makes people uncomfortable and or perhaps a bore. Keep yourself from sharing the negative events in your life.

Meeting new people and having to make conversation is not everyone's favorite thing, but if you follow these ten steps and do not forget that you are working as an Executive Chauffeur, and be yourself, you might find yourself enjoying more of your passengers.

Source: https://www.psychologytoday.com/us/blog/fulfillment-any-age/201107/10-tips-talk-about-anything-anyone Author: Susan Krauss Whitbourne, Ph.D. 2011.

De-escalating a Customer

It is inevitable that problems will arise during the process of servicing a client so you as a professional should be able to deescalate situations and change directions from negative outcomes to positive outcomes!

Here are three things that you can do to immediately deescalate situations with customers.

1. **Create calm**

Create calm by using anti-inflammatory words and reasoning with the client so that the client feels that fixing the problem is just as important to you as it is to them.

Example:

"I'm sorry you've had such a frustrating experience."

"Thank you for letting me know about this issue. I will make sure it gets corrected!"

These statements show the customer that you are on their side and that they can trust you.

2. **Assertively take charge**

If your customer continues to use inflammatory language and insists on being intense, you must take charge of the situation.

Example:

"I'm trying to help, but if you continue to yell and swear, I am going to have to direct you to upper management and distance myself from this issue."

"I am sorry, it is impossible for me to help you while listening to that language. If it stops, I can help."

"I want to help you, yet the language is getting in the way."

Taking charge of the situation helps you stay in control of the outcome.

3. **Move the interaction forward**

After you have created calm and taken charge of the situation, you let them know how you are taking steps to fix the problem.

Example:

"What I'll do is let management know what the issue is and have them fix it as soon as possible so that it won't happen again."

This final step is crucial to diverting the customer's focus into a better situation and move on from the problem so that you can continue to work towards a positive experience for the client.

VEHICLE

Always remember that the first few seconds will dictate the rest, so your vehicle should match the type of first impression that you want to impose, but it should also be of a kind that can cater to different clients wants and needs.

Standards

In today's world, it is difficult to choose the right vehicle for a Chauffeur due to the immense number of brands and classes of vehicles. Not only the type of vehicle and client experience is important, but the Chauffeur's taste also comes into this equation.

- Your vehicle should be of black color with black interior unless you are driving a specialty vehicle such as a high value vehicle, an old classic vehicle or the customer's vehicle or if you are driving a stretched limousine.
- Your vehicle should have all gear necessary for emergencies, such as a fire extinguisher, spare tire, and tools.
- Your vehicle should have all proper licenses, documentations, and certifications so that you can work efficiently without worrying about any legal issues and liabilities.
- Your vehicle should be up to date with maintenance so that you can avoid unwanted breakdowns.
- Your vehicle should have plenty of leg room and headroom for tall passengers.
- Your vehicle should have a large enough trunk for extra-large items.
- Your vehicle should have a large tank of gas so that you can travel long distances without having to make frequent stops at gas stations.
- Your vehicle should have proper cup holders for the driver and the customers to avoid spillage.

- Your vehicle should have good quality sound system that is set to low with mellow, positive, calming music set to your client's preferences but can also provide loud quality sound for entertainment.
- Your vehicle should have a working toll tag for non-stop tolls so that you can save money and expedite continuation of travel.

Service Standards

Regardless of what system you or your company utilize to keep the vehicle clean, a Chauffeur is the last checkpoint to a vehicles cleanliness. If the weather does not permit the outside of your vehicle to stay clean, you must pay special attention to the inside.

- Your vehicle should be odorless. (Use deodorizer, NO scented freshener)
- Your vehicle should be squeaky clean, both inside and outside. (No coffee stains, dust, crumbs, food remains etc.)
- Your vehicle should be noise free. (No rattles, ringing, or scraping)
- Always make sure you have a full tank of gas, but also make sure that there is no spillage.
- Always make sure to check your vehicle after a client leaves.

You never know when they might leave something behind. If they leave illegal substances in the vehicle, contact your superior, discard it in the garbage or turn it into the police. Your vehicle is often sniffed by police dogs, so always be prepared or you might get into trouble with the law even though you are only doing your job.

Knowledge

It is imperative that you know everything about your vehicle so that you do not get caught in unexpected situations.

- You must know how to control your Infotainment system, Bluetooth, navigation system, temperature controls, etc.
- You must know how to reset and reboot the electronic systems of your vehicle.
- You must know how to change your vehicle's tire in case you get a flat.
- You must know how to operate your vehicle in a safe manner.
- You must know how to get a battery boost from a donor vehicle.
- You must know how to operate your vehicles traction control.

Handling Luggage

It is important to note that most of your trips will not involve dealing with large amounts of luggage. However, it is important for you to know how to service clients that come with various amounts of luggage or gear. Most clients who are traveling to and from airports will have a couple of bags to put in the trunk plus their personal item such as briefcase or backpack.

People are very defensive when you try to handle their personal items, so you have to ask them if they would like to put all of their items in the trunk or keep it with them. As you probably know, it is always a hassle getting into a vehicle with your hands full, so you must offer to hold their personal item while they get in the vehicle. You can also tell them that you will place it on the other seat for them.

When you get to the destination. Pickup their personal items from the passenger seat for the passenger and hand it over on their side of the vehicle. Doing this simple act of service will show your level of care and professionalism, but you have to be mindful of the client's preferences and demeanor towards your actions so that you don't seem pushy or intrusive.

On the other hand, loading a vehicle with a large amount of luggage can be very intimidating, but if you follow these guidelines, you will have a higher rate of success in this area.

- Always lay out all the luggage in front of you before loading so that you can properly pick larger and heavier items to load first.

- Place items in the trunk, NEVER throw passengers' belongings into the vehicle.
- Start with the heaviest items on the bottom because it helps keep the center of gravity of the vehicle low, doing this will help maintain control of the vehicle. It also prevents the heavyweight items from damaging lighter items.
- If the vehicle is large enough, put a large piece of luggage on its side and standing vertically, doing this will help maximize space usage and create a platform to add more luggage on top.
- Smaller items that are on the top layer of luggage should be properly secured so that it does not slide forward in case of harsh breaking, doing this will avoid passengers getting hurt from loose objects moving through the vehicle.
- If you are driving a sedan, analyze the amount of space needed to fit the luggage. Sometimes larger items will prevent smaller items from fitting, so put the large item in the front seat if unoccupied and all the smaller pieces in the trunk.
- When unloading, make sure that you do not throw the passengers' belongings on the floor. Always place it with care, since you do not know if there are fragile items inside.
- Always pickup items with care so that you do not damage the vehicle or get hurt doing so.

VAN

SUV

SEDAN

Amenities

Amenities are used to stand out from the crowd and create an unforgettable experience for the client. All amenities in the vehicle are for the client and not for you. Clients that get the special treatment with the amenities are more likely to request you as a Chauffeur on the next job. The following are examples of amenities that can be added to the vehicle.

- Premium water
- Phone chargers (IOS & Android)
- Mints or premium candy
- Tissue dispenser with plenty of tissues in it
- Napkins
- Magazines and/or newspapers
- Wi-Fi
- Umbrella
- Pen and paper
- Lighter/matches
- Hand sanitizer
- Disposable masks
- Disposable gloves

Tools

The tools that a Chauffeur carries are highly subjective to his or her experience and ability to problem solve. The following list is an example of what I personally think is necessary for my daily activities as an Executive Chauffeur.

- Black cooler with pockets
  - (Napkins, utensils, beverages, and food)
- Black bag with many pockets
  - Multi-tool
  - Microfiber cloths
  - Extra cell phone chargers and battery pack
  - Cellphone holder
  - Medicine
  - Deodorizer
  - Mouth hygiene kit (tooth brush, tooth paste, mouth wash and dental floss)
  - Pens and notebook
  - Gloves
  - Sewing kit
  - Emergency kit
  - Spare clothes
  - Adhesive tape
  - Laptop or tablet
  - Book
  - Hat
  - Flashlight
  - Tripod/Selfie stick to take pictures of clients upon their request
  - Trash bag

- Roadside emergency kit
- Reflective triangles or flares
- Electrical jump cables
- Mini sweeping broom and shovel
- Watch
- Sunglasses
- Pocket knife
- Personal protection tools (pepper spray, taser, pistol etc.)
- Biohazard kit

CHECKLIST

Exterior Damage/Cleanliness ______.

Bumpers______. Fenders______. Doors______. Hood______.
Roof______. Lights______. Wipers______. Tires______.
Breaks______. Exhaust______. Mechanical______. Other______.

Interior Damage/Cleanliness ______.

Horn______. Flashers______. Radio______. Lights______.
Camera______. Leather______. Locks______. Handles______.
Noise______. Heat / AC______. Oil level______. Keys______.
Phone______. iPad______. Gas level______. Documents ______.
Cashless Toll Tag ______.

Observations:

____

____

____

Amenities

- ☐ Premium water
- ☐ Phone chargers (IOS & Android)
- ☐ Mints and premium candy
- ☐ Tissue dispenser with plenty of tissues in it
- ☐ Napkins
- ☐ Magazines and or newspapers
- ☐ Wi-Fi
- ☐ Umbrella
- ☐ Pen and Paper
- ☐ Lighter / Matches
- ☐ Hand sanitizer
- ☐ Disposable Masks
- ☐ Disposable Gloves

Tools

- [ ] Black cooler with pockets
    - [ ] (Napkins, utensils, beverages, and food)
- [ ] Black bag with many pockets
    - [ ] Multitool
    - [ ] Microfiber cloths
    - [ ] Extra cell phone chargers and battery pack
    - [ ] Cellphone holder
    - [ ] Medicine
    - [ ] Deodorizer
    - [ ] Mouth hygiene kit (tooth brush, tooth paste, mouth wash and dental floss)
    - [ ] Pens and Notebook
    - [ ] Gloves
    - [ ] Sewing kit
    - [ ] Medical Emergency kit
    - [ ] Spare clothes
    - [ ] Adhesive Tape
    - [ ] Laptop or Tablet
    - [ ] Book
    - [ ] Hat
    - [ ] Compact Rechargeable Flashlight
    - [ ] Tripod / Selfie stick to take pictures of clients
    - [ ] Portable inverter
    - [ ] Trash bag
- [ ] Roadside emergency kit
- [ ] Reflective triangles or flares
- [ ] Electrical jump cables
- [ ] Mini sweeping broom and shovel
- [ ] Watch
- [ ] Sunglasses
- [ ] Pocket knife
- [ ] Personal protection tools (pepper spray, taser, pistol etc...)
- [ ] Biohazard Kit

8

FOCUS

A Chauffeur's focus should be entirely on what the client wants and will pay for. No matter which client you are taking care of, they essentially want the highest level of service. Focus on the task at hand. It is especially important for you to pay attention to all the details involved in that task. Every detail is so important that it dictates the result so, practice until it becomes second nature.

The easiest way to become proficient at the job is to build one job related habit at a time. On average, it takes between ten and fifteen days of repetitiveness to create a habit. Use this to your advantage as you can use these habits as building blocks to professionalism in your career.

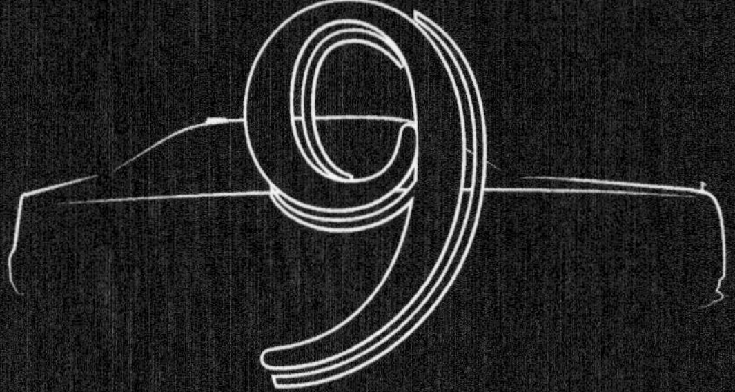

9

TRIP DETAILS

The difference between good service and great service is the attention to detail. To create something exceptional, your mindset must be relentlessly focused on the smallest details.

Time of pickup

It is extremely important for you to be on time (at least 15 minutes early) in case of an unexpected event when in-route.

Location of pickup

You must know where to pick up or meet your passenger so that you can time yourself properly. Note any specific details of where pickup location is for future reference.

Number of passengers

So that you know how many people to look for and if you have large enough vehicle to fit every passenger.

Passenger's full name

Google your passengers and find out what they look like and any other information to be used in potential conversion, such as job description, country of origin, language, affiliations, interest, etc. This also avoids missing the passenger in a crowded situation.

Any special requests

Many clients have special requests such as, newspapers, magazines, radio station preference, vehicle type, coffee, and a car seat for a child, to name a few.

Destination

You must know in advance, how long it will take to arrive at the destination and where exactly to drop off the passenger.

Event information

It is important to know the schedule of the events that your passengers will be attending so that you can co-ordinate the travel time properly. Example of events: dinner reservations, meetings, flights, theater shows, concerts, games, etc.

Clients contact information.

Passengers are often late! You must text or call your clients to let them know you have arrived.

Example: (Hello Mr. John Doe, this is your Chauffeur Alisson. I am ready at your convenience. Please confirm this massage. ETA to airport Is 45 minutes.)

Greeter or assistants

You must have proper communication with greeters and assistants that might be coordinating schedules.

10

DRIVING

Driving can be satisfying, or it can be terrifying. Driving for yourself is completely different from driving for a client. When driving for yourself, you have many liberties that you would not otherwise have when driving for a client, so here are some points on how you can turn your driving into a customer focused driving experience.

Always make sure to have a full tank of gas.

(It Is essential to be prepared for any length trip and it is only permissible to stop for gas with a client on board if you are traveling so far that you will run out of gas before arriving at the destination.)

Obey all traffic laws, independent of your client's requests.

(If you break the law, you can lose your driver's license, if you lose your license, you cannot drive, if you cannot drive, you cannot work!)

(Look for your local traffic laws book at the DMV and study it.)

Sometimes, Chauffeurs are inclined to satisfy or help clients in certain situations and that can have unbelievably bad repercussions. Here is an example of how I put my life situation on the line for a customer who was running late for an important meeting and received no additional benefit from doing so.

I had picked up a corporate lawyer from his private jet at a private FBO. He entered the vehicle in a rush and asked me to drive as fast as possible to the destination. He continuously made comments such as "I'm sorry for making you rush, but I will lose the client if I don't get there in time!" I felt bad for the customer and proceeded to speed towards the destination. We arrived on location, and he rushed into the meeting. I waited around the office until he was done and then took him to the hotel. The client acted as if nothing had happened, got out of the car, and didn't even say thank you!

Moral of the story is that I risked my life and his life by speeding and potentially getting into an accident. I risked getting pulled over by a police officer and getting in trouble with the law. I also risked my job and equipment, and I could have negatively affected many people's lives just because I wanted to help a client. Therefore, taking all that risk is never worth any potential of bigger tips, reviews, or referrals!

Know your routes before picking up your client.

(Clients expect you to know where you are going so that you do not lose time researching routes when they are in the vehicle.) Have your GPS set. It is also important to know the ins and outs of the area that you are in so that if your client is in a hurry, you can cut through parking garages, use service roads and back alleys to get around traffic as long as it is safe to do so.

The ride should be as smooth as possible.

(Clients pay for comfort). "Drive as if you have a bucket of water on your hood and you can't spill the water from the bucket!"

Your accelerations should be smooth and consistent, with no jolting motions.

Your breaking should be light and consistent with no jerking motions. (Glide to a stop)

Radio

Your radio should be off or set to low and to the station of the client's preference.

(Clients often are focused and do not want distractions.)

Navigation

If you are using a GPS, Navigation System, WAZE, GOOGLE MAPS, etc.... always have it ready before your client gets in the vehicle and always have it visible to the client to avoid route questioning.

Feeling safe

Vehicle doors should be locked when the client is inside.

(Clients need to feel protected)

Drive defensively!

(Always have a way out, avoid being trapped with your vehicle. Your clients are often of high profile and sometimes require an extra safety measure.)

Stay far enough from the vehicle in front of you in case you must break suddenly. Be aware of your surroundings.

Driving with security

High-profile clients often travel with personal bodyguards. Security personnel usually travel in the front seat and are always on alert. Make them feel safe by driving defensively and try to keep the car moving as much as you can, but always give yourself plenty of room to escape from any possible situation.

Driving in a motorcade

Many public figures or high-profile clients travel with multiple people and request a motorcade situation. The main client should always be in the middle of the motorcade, but if there is only two vehicles, then he/she should be in the lead vehicle. Always lookout for potential danger on the road and always keep the vehicles together when traveling. Always protect the other vehicles by making space for them to merge and or park. Always maintain visual with all vehicles.

Parking

Always park your vehicle with the minimum number of maneuvers.

Never make your clients step in water, dirt, or potholes when getting in and out of the vehicle. During bad weather, make sure your client has a solid footing when entering or exiting the vehicle.

Always make it as easy as possible for your client to get in and out of the vehicle.

Your client should always enter and exit the vehicle on the curb side to keep them safe.

Phone usage

Do not use your phone unless absolutely necessary. See your local laws and rulings on this topic for better reference.

(Phones are a distraction and you need to be focused on the job. Use your Bluetooth in case of emergencies.)

Keep your car clean

Avoid driving through dirty places and getting your vehicle dirty.

(Your vehicle must be always presentable.)

Be a professional driver

(Be on time and drive efficiently to be on time!)

Seatbelt

Wear a seatbelt and encourage your passengers to do it as well!

(Wearing a seatbelt will increase your chances of surviving an accident and will avoid fines.)

In case of an accident

Give special attention to your client. If your client is not hurt, exchange documentation with the other person involved. Take record of the scene of the accident by taking pictures and video of the scene. File the police report online later instead of waiting for the police to show up. Do it all as fast as possible. If the collision is on the highway and everyone is ok and both vehicles are drivable, pull off on the next exit to exchange documents. (If you stay on the highway, you will receive a ticket for obstruction of traffic.)

SERVICE PROCESS

Clients and passenger are all different but they also have many similarities because you are dealing with the personal attributes on the difference side but you are dealing with similarities on the task at hand side. There are 4 main procedures when serving a client. These procedures are a simplified guide to servicing a client. Many times, parts of these procedures will mix orders and require you to analyze and adapt to the situation.

Initial Procedure

This all happens outside the vehicle.

- Arrive at least 15 minutes early.
- Make sure there is a comfortable temperature in the car.
- Make sure the radio is set to low with the client's favorite station on.
- Contact your client via TEXT or Phone Call. (Make sure the clients name is spelled correctly.)

TEXT: "Hello Mr./Ms./Mrs. Smith, this is your Chauffeur Alisson. I am ready to pick you up at your convenience. Please confirm this message and contact me when you are ready. Current ETA to (airport, restaurant, theater, etc....) is approximately 43 minutes."

CALL: "Hello Mr./Ms./Mrs. Smith, this is your Chauffeur Alisson. I am ready to pick you up at your convenience. Current ETA to (airport, restaurant, theatre, etc....) is approximately 43 minutes. See you soon!

- If they ask for you to wait or tell you that they are running late;

Always tell them: (No worries, I'm here for your convenience.)

- When your client arrives:

Open the vehicle's door for your client. Always open the door for the ladies first. (Hello Mr./Ms./Mrs. Smith,

I'm your Chauffeur Alisson. How are you today?) Listen to their answer.

Put their luggage in the trunk before they enter the vehicle. Usually, the passengers will leave you with the luggage and enter the vehicle while you are handling their luggage.

DO NOT SLAM THE TRUNK SHUT! Close it firmly.

Close the passenger's door once they are inside the vehicle.

DO NOT SLAM THE DOOR SHUT! Close it firmly.

- Make sure they did not drop anything on the floor.
- Get in the driver's seat DO NOT SLAM THE DOOR SHUT! Close it firmly.
- Lock all doors.

Second Procedure

This all happens inside the vehicle.

- You: "I'd like to confirm that we are headed to (airport, restaurant, theatre, etc....), is that correct?"

  Client: "Yes, that is correct ,"

  You: "Great! We will arrive in 43minutes."

  Client: "Thanks"

- Tell your clients about all the amenities

  "You'll find water, mints, tissues, magazines, hand sanitizer, gloves and a phone charger for you to use; and the Wi-Fi login and password is ... "

- Communicate with your dispatch, let them know you have

  (POB) Passenger On Board (CIC) Customer In Car

- You: "Do you have everything with you, and you are not forgetting anything before I start driving?"
- Client: "I'm not forgetting anything, let's go!"

Third Procedure

This all happens while in transit.

- Have a polite conversation with your client if time is appropriate and if they are open to It.
- Say their name at least once during the conversation.
- Update them with arrival time when you are ten minutes away from the destination.
- Towards the end of the trip, start selling!

Last Procedure

This all happens while in transit.

- Mr./Ms. Smith we have arrived.
- Open the door for your client. (Always open or close the doors for females first!) Remember, do not slam the door when closing it.
- Sell, Sell, Sell: "It was a pleasure driving for you, Mr./ Ms. Smith. Here is my business card, you can always request me as your Chauffeur."
- "Don't forget any of your belongings in the car!".
- Check the back seat for any lost items.
- Get the vehicle ready for your next client. (Take out any trash, sanitize the vehicle, shake the mats, fill up the gas tank, turn the radio off, etc.)
- TEXT all of your clients at the end of your shift.

("Dear Mr./Ms. Smith, this is your Chauffeur, Alisson. It was a pleasure driving for you today. Please remember to refer our services to all of your friends and remember you can always request me as your Chauffeur. Enjoy the rest of your day!")

Dealing with Stinky Passengers

Sometimes people go through situations that leave them with less desirable odors and it is the job of an Executive Chauffeur to be discreet. In some cases, people may have been traveling for a long period without time for a shower, not having brushed their teeth or have consumed foods that cause flatulence. These are just a few situations that an Executive Chauffeurs encounter periodically.

If you are exposed to such situation, it is your job to make the best of the situation without embarrassing or insulting the passenger. The absolute best way to deal with such situations is to just stay quiet and ignore the odors. But sometimes you can speak your mind to solve the problem if it is to the benefit of the client.

Here are five examples that might help you relate when such things happen.

The first example is when I was assigned to pick up a gentleman at the airport and take him directly to a restaurant. After meeting him at the airport and picking up his luggage, we headed to the car. He asked about how much time it would take to get to the restaurant because he did not want to be late for his date. I told him it would take about thirty-five minutes. When we got into the car, I noticed that stench coming from the back seat. So, I asked him for the time of his reservation and he told me that he had about twenty minutes to spare. I asked him if he would like to stop at a close by hotel to use the restroom to freshen up. I also told him that a specific hotel had complimentary hygiene products in their lounge bathroom. He took the hint and said, "Yes, that's a great idea,". He had recognized that he smelled terrible after an eleven-hour flight. He went inside, changed clothes, brushed his teeth, combed his hair, and used some deodorant spray. He came back to the car, and we arrived on time for his date. At the end of the day, I sent him a text message thanking him for the opportunity to drive for him. He responded by thanking me for stopping at the hotel because he was sure that his date would not have liked the stinky man that had just got off of a long flight. He said that my actions made all the difference in the outcome of that date and sent me a very generous tip as gratitude.

The second example is from when I was dispatched to pick up a very classy-looking business woman from a restaurant and take her home. She was very classy around her peers and acted very professionally as she hopped into my vehicle. I greeted her and went on to talk about the restaurant that she had dinner at. She mentioned that the food was incredible, but she ate too much of everything. Unfortunately, the food she ate did not do her much good, because it caused her to become very gassy. In the middle of the trip, she started releasing the rotten gasses from inside her bowel and it stunk up the entire car. She was very embarrassed at the situation, but did not say anything. I ignored the bad smell, but I could not tolerate that smell for much longer. I turned on the AC and the air circulation in the vehicle and she immediately asked to open the windows and proceeded to say " I wonder when they will finish working on these sewer lines?" I just said "hopefully soon!". Yes, she lied. But at the end of the day, the problem was resolved without embarrassing or exposing the client. She gave me a nice tip, and I got a good laugh after I dropped her off.

The third example is about a trip situation that took maturity and compassion to deal with. I was assigned to go pick up an elderly lady at her senior living community home and take her to her doctor's appointment, then back home. When I arrived at the pickup location, she greeted me with a big smile as she pushed her walker towards the car. I helped her get settled in the seat and fasten her seatbelt. I placed her walker in the trunk and proceeded to taking her to the doctor's office. When we arrived, she soiled her adult diaper while getting out of the vehicle. There was no need to say anything! I just helped her get out of the car and got her inside the doctor's office. I aired out the car while I waited and then proceeded to taking her back home after her appointment. Fortunately, there was no mess to clean up and, as you can see, ignoring the problem and being compassionate can be the best way to deal with a client.

The fourth example is about a wedding party that I was assigned to service on a Saturday morning. I got the stretched limousine ready with all the required equipment and requested amenities and headed to the pickup location. When I arrived, the groom and the groomsman came to greet me and board the limousine. Unfortunately, the groom unknowingly stepped on some dog feces while walking to the limo. They boarded the limo and immediately started calling each other out as responsible for the stench. It was comical! I was having a blast listening to all the comments. However, it got to a point where we had to get the problem resolved. As they got out of the limo at the drop off location, I told them to check the bottom of their shoes and sure enough, the groom was the one responsible for a stinky ride. I gave him a bottle of water and some paper towels to clean up with and the problem was solved.

This situation goes to show that you don't have to make comments, but you do have to help solve the problem.

The fifth and last example is to show how sometimes you can be the problem. I had a client who was very happy with my services and kept me on the clock 24 hours a day. I had little time to go home and freshen up. During one very hot day in NYC, we kept the windows open for the client's delight, but, unfortunately for me, I was wearing a suit. The heat got the best of me and I started to stink! I looked through my Chauffeur bag for some deodorant or body spray so I could mask the odor, but I had failed to replenish what I had used. When the clients closed the windows, my unpleasant body odor engulfed the entire vehicle, making it unbearable. The clients complained about it and unfortunately but understandably, I never heard from them again.

As you can observe, undesirable odors are part of our lives and regardless of where you are, it is just a matter of time before you encounter such odors. It is the job of an Executive Chauffeur to have proper etiquette and knowledge to know how to deal with these types of situations without insulting or embarrassing your passengers and be prepared for your own mishaps.

Dealing with Drunk Passengers

It is very normal to service passenger who have had a few drinks during a meal or have been bar hopping. So, it is important to know how to handle drunk individuals.

As an Executive Chauffeur you will rarely be exposed to extremely drunk passengers. Nonetheless, you will encounter situations where you, as the sober person, need to be able to handle such passengers.

It is acceptable for your passengers to have fun and enjoy alcoholic beverages but there are limits or boundaries that you as the service provider need to set. If you identify your passengers are trespassing the limits of being sober enough to make sane decisions, you must set the boundaries. Make it clear to them that if there is any risk to their safety, your safety, damage to property or disturbance of peace, the services will be terminated immediately.

If you see that your clients have had too much to drink, keep barf bags handy in case they vomit. It is better for the passenger to vomit in a barf bag than expose other passengers to the mess. A barf bag will prevent you from having to deal with a dirty mess, prevent biohazard exposure and cleanup fees that may incur. Always carry a wet rag and a dry rag that can be used to cleanup an unexpected mess.

Always evaluate the entry and exit access point to the vehicle so that you can minimize the risk of injury to the passengers. People who are drunk, have their motor skills impaired, so having a clear path is essential to prevent injuries.

Once you have identified that your passenger is drunk, make sure that you do not confront him or her directly. Be as friendly as possible, create common ground and use the tactics of de-escalating a customer. Doing this will help keep the drunk person from becoming aggressive and will help you complete your service faster.

If you have set your clear boundaries and your passengers exceed the limits, you can terminate service whenever you feel necessary. Contact the police if you feel unsafe and encounter resistance or aggressiveness from your passengers.

Sometimes, you will be transporting minors on birthday parties, school games, homecoming events, proms, graduations etc. Servicing minors involves greater responsibility and has a higher liability risk since a responsible adult is not always present. It is encouraged that when introducing yourself, mention while the adult is present that underage drinking of alcoholic beverages will not be tolerated under any circumstances. If any of the minors get caught drinking alcoholic beverages inside the vehicle, the services will be paused or terminated immediately. The responsible adult will have to accompany the minors and the police will be contacted.

Setting these expectations and clear boundaries will prevent you from being liable for your passengers' irresponsible actions. It will also keep you from being blamed for supplying alcoholic beverages to minors.

Always remember that your safety and the safety of your passengers is the most important part of your service.

Servicing a Funeral

Death is part of life and unfortunately in this industry, we are exposed to it much more frequently than in other professions. You, as an Executive Chauffeur, should be able to act accordingly when servicing a funeral.

You should be wearing a Chauffeur uniform, which was designed to be appropriate for most of the events that you will be attending. I encourage you to not wear a hat at funerals so that you can convey an image of respect. I do encourage you to wear sunglasses so that you can disguise the direction of where you are looking and avoid eye contact that encourages engagement.

Funerals can be challenging to service, since it involves a tremendous amount of emotional control. You will be engaging with people who are hurting emotionally and are extremely sensitive so, minimize your engagement with people, but always show kindness and be as accommodating as possible.

It is polite to say "I cannot relate to the pain that you are going through but, if there is anything that I can do, please don't hesitate to tell me." Or it can be a simple phrase such as, "I'm so sorry for your loss!"

Once you are done paying your respects, mind your own business! Stay out of the way of people who are either there for the service or to service.

After the funeral service is over, and the coffin is loaded into the hearse. It is common for the family of the deceased to ride in the limo with you, so you must be as comforting as possible. No music in the vehicle. If you are driving a vehicle with party lights, they must be turned off or be in the white setting. Tissues and water should be provided to your passengers.

(If you want to go above and beyond for your client, have a supply of snacks in the vehicle because people forget to eat due to emotional stress or are unprepared for such long events.)

When following the hearse, keep a close distance, but also pay very close attention to your surroundings. Funeral procession escort vehicles will be moving all around you and directing traffic. You also must be mindful of other motorists that are not in the procession and might not respect the procession.

When arriving at the cemetery, follow directions to the burial site. Be respectful of the property and avoid riding or stepping on tombstones. Follow the standard procedure of opening doors and assisting with entering and exiting the vehicle. During the burial, it is respectful to stand outside your vehicle by the door that is facing the burial site.

After the burial, proceed with normal service to the drop off location.

Once you have finished servicing the client, do not forget to follow up with a text message.

Example: "Hi Mr. /Mrs. Smith, I am just passing by to thank you for trusting me with such an important event in your life. I ask that you please leave an online review so that I can continue to get more amazing clients such as yourself. If there is anything you need, please don't hesitate to contact me. My prayers go out to you and your family. Have a blessed day!"

Now that we have talked about providing excellent service at a funeral, we must talk about your own emotions at a funeral. You must be prepared to contain your emotions since you might relate to the situation or encounter undesirable circumstances. It is very normal to service the funeral of a person who lived to be ninety years old but, it is not common to service the funeral of a one-year-old that has passed due to illness or an unfortunate accident.

Bottom line is that you will be exposed to intense, emotional events. So, you must be emotionally intelligent so that you can maintain your emotional health. Do not hesitate to share these traumatic experiences so that people can help you navigate through such emotions.

Dealing with Injury

In rare occurrences, a Chauffeur will be exposed to an injury or must deal with an injured client. It is important that you, as a professional, are prepared to deal with such situations.

If you are injured while servicing a client, you must gauge the severity of your injury. The severity of your injury will determine if you will continue service or terminate service to take care of yourself. In such case, if you have a supervisor, you must contact him or her immediately and make them aware of the situation. Your supervisor will take the necessary steps to deal with the client and you can proceed with taking care of your injury.

If your client/passenger is injured while you are servicing him or her, you must follow the following steps.

Step 1: Seek medical attention for the injured party

The first thing you need to do in the event of an accident is get medical treatment right away. Never underestimate the severity of an injury.

If the injury is very clearly superficial, such as a small cut, assist in the care for the injury by offering access to your first aid kit. But, still encourage your client to get checked out by their health provider as soon as possible.

It is highly encouraged that you, as the Executive Chauffeur, be CPR trained and certified so that you can give the best care to the injured person.

Step 2: Apologize but do not admit fault

Simply say "I'm sorry this happened!" Never admit that you knew there was a problem ahead of time, even if you did. Promise to fix the problem promptly but never say anything that could be taken as admitting responsibility.

Step 3: Inspect the area where your customer was injured

Once you have ensured that your client is okay or they are on their way to the hospital, look at where the accident occurred. See if you can find any obvious causes of the incident, such as a wet floor, shards of glass, or an exposed sharp object.

Take pictures and notes of what you find, so that you have evidence to refer to in the event that your client decides to file a lawsuit against you or your business.

If you do notice any hazards, fix it right away to prevent similar injuries from happening in the future.

Step 4: Collect witness statements and create an incident report

If anyone saw the accident take place, ask them for statements and contact information (if you do not already have it).

It is also a good idea to put together an incident report to record what happened. This should be a standard document that all employees have access to and know how to fill out in the event of an accident. You can include any witness statements you collect in this report.

Incident report form can also be found online.

Step 5: Contact your insurance provider and your attorney

The final step is if a customer gets hurt on company property or by using any of the company's equipment is to get in touch with your insurance company and your attorney. At this point, your insurer and attorney will likely take over and contact your client on your behalf.

Customer Relationship Boundaries

While being exposed to countless clients and passengers, an Executive Chauffeur will often be offered to join, Parties, Dinners, and Social Events, and here lies an ambiguous dilemma. To accept or decline the clients offers?

For many years, industry standard was to politely decline any offers made by the client or passenger. But as technology and customs evolved, this rule has also evolved. Back in the old days it was customary for drivers to have the absolute responsibility to always stay with the vehicle so that the vehicle was always safe and ready for the client.

Today these same rules apply but because of technology a Chauffeur has more freedom when it comes to leaving the vehicle in a safe place but unattended for some controlled time.

It is undeniable that the Executive Chauffeur along with his vehicle are the one common safety anchor for clients, especially when servicing groups. The vehicle can be the main meeting point in case the group gets separated and the driver can assist with any unforeseen needs.

The question now becomes, how to define the fine line between being professional and courteous to abusive and intrusive when the Chauffeur is offered to join an event? It takes great discernment to make the right decision!

In general, when accepting an invitation from a client, you must be sure that you will not seem intrusive or abusive of the situation. Try to make your decision based on the answers to the following questions:

1. Will the vehicle be safe if you leave it unattended? The answer to this question is purely based on location. Consider the surroundings, accessibility, supporting safety such as guards and gates, and weather.
2. Can I get back to the vehicle before the client / passenger if you leave the vehicle unattended? You must set expectations with your client / passenger and stay in contact so you do not get caught by surprise.
3. How fast can you get back to the vehicle and have it ready in case of an emergency? Give yourself ample time to get back to the vehicle and have it running with enough time to get the temperature back to the client / passenger's likings.
4. Can you get the food and eat it in the vehicle instead of eating with the clients or guests? It is very convenient for you to take the food back to the vehicle and eat it away from the client / passenger. This will help you avoid unwanted and uncomfortable situations that could ruin the relationship.
5. Can you finish eating and get back to the vehicle before the client / passenger finishes their meal? If you are eating inside with the client / passenger, make sure that you politely finish first and head back to the vehicle with the excuse that you must be there to protect the vehicle.
6. Can you be friendly and intentional with the purpose of networking for new and continuous business if you accept the invitation to an event? Use these op-

portunities to prospect for new clients and solidify relationships with current clients / passengers.

7. Can you fulfill any requests while fraternizing in the premises? The drawback of being away from the vehicle is that if the client / passenger asks you for anything that was left in vehicle or for you to run an arrand, you will be taking more time to accomplish that request.
8. Will you jeopardize the relationship in any form if you accept an invitation? Clients / passengers will often make offers as a sign of respect and politeness. You must be able to distinguish a true invite vs. an act of kindness. If the client doesn't insist at least three times, politely decline their offer.
9. Will the person who made the offer be offended if you decline the offer? Sometimes it is disrespectful to the client if you decline their offer, so, be mindful that different cultures behave in different ways.

Take into consideration who will be paying for such privilege. Companies will often buy tickets in bulk so leftover tickets are ok to be used.

Private dinner parties are also paid for in advance with a predetermined amount of food or head count so enjoying these circumstances are perfectly acceptable if you can identify that there is enough for everyone before you get your share.

Here are a few examples to learn from:

a. You are taking a couple to a restaurant where they will be celebrating their anniversary. They ask that you join them. Should you accept? The right answer is to politely decline. But if that same couple offers you a meal to be brought to you at the car so you can eat while waiting for them. Still politely decline and if they insist, you accept.

b. You are a male Chauffeur driving a limousine filled with female passengers, going to a club. They ask you to join them. Should you accept? The right answer is to politely decline. You as a male will be invading their personal space as females have a totally different way of having fun than men do. You would also be faced with the challenge of leaving your limo unattended in questionable places that have too much foot traffic.

c. You are taking a large group of passengers to a private party that is being held at a private venue. They ask you to join them when the food is served. Should you accept? The right answer is to politely decline if the event has a small enough amount of people where you will stand out if you go inside. If the event is being attended by a very large group where your presence will not make a difference, discretely go get some food and eat in the vehicle. During large occupancy events, it is much easier to get free food if you get in touch with the catering staff or coordinator but you must be mindful that getting free food is a privilege and not a right.

d. You are servicing a group of bachelors who are celebrating the engagement of one of their friends. You take them bar hoping and they come back to the vehicle under the influence of alcohol and ask you to take them to a strip club. Once there, they ask you to join them for the fun. Should you accept? The right answer is no. Strip clubs are usually located in bad areas where, leaving the vehicle unattended could lead to damage to the vehicle. The boundaries of service would also be breached since you would be involved in sexual actions and communication with the clients. Participating in their personal fun will jeopardize future requests since they would not want to be judged on the next time that they ask for this type of service.

Always remember that your primary job as an Executive Chauffeur is to serve and not be served!

12

SELLING

There is no business without any sales.

If you are a professional Chauffeur, you soon understand that SALES rule the limo service business. The sooner you turn the Chauffeuring Service into a proactive process of understanding customers wants and needs, the more money you will make by selling your service and expertise.

True Executive Chauffeurs understand that they are the face of the company and that their perceived image out in the world is the company's marketing and selling strategy. Therefore, an Executive Chauffeur is the most important asset for any company.

In this section, you will learn about the qualities of a salesperson, the skills that a successful salesperson have, the steps to a successful sale, scripts that can be used during service and using social media to promote yourself and your business.

Qualities of a Sales Person

Audacity

Audacity means that you have the willingness to take bold risks, and being audacious in this industry is a must if you want to be successful. There are many opportunities to be audacious as an Executive Chauffeur.

You might consider being audacious when waiting for a passenger and if it's a business location. You may try to enter the premises of where they are, scout the area for potential future customers, locate bathrooms, locate lounge areas, locate free food etc. but, if you are not audacious enough to go inside and talk to people, you might not take advantage of these opportunities unless the passenger invites you in.

Keep in mind that you must know the limits of being audacious and intrusive. Because sometimes your audacity may take you places where you are not welcome and ruin your potential opportunities or current situation. As a rule of thumb, refrain from entering enclosed locations where private events are being held or where small groups of people are meeting.

It is extremely important that you apply the tips of communication that we reviewed in the communication section so that you can maintain an acceptable level of audacity while not being intrusive.

Repetition

Repetition is the key to creating habits and the more you repeat the process of servicing a client, the better you will be at it. It is encouraged that you repeat your story, presentation, or sales pitch as many times as possible so that you will get to a point where selling yourself and your services becomes natural and spontaneous.

Repetition will make your sales efforts look effortless and not seem as if you are a pushy salesperson.

Your preparation process should be repeated.

Your service process should be repeated.

Your sales process should be repeated.

Your follow-up process should be repeated.

Discipline

Discipline is the willingness to apply repetition so that you can identify flaws, adapt, and adjust your story, presentation, or sales pitch. It takes discipline to repeat your preparation process. It takes discipline to repeat your service process. It takes discipline to repeat your sales process. It takes discipline to repeat your follow-up process. Without discipline, you will be going around in circles and never accomplish any growth.

Intuition

Intuition is the ability to qualify your prospect or leads before you pitch yourself or your services. Intuition produces a series of questions to find out if your lead or prospect is a potential or continuous client. You will be identifying the type of client through conversation or observation. This will show if the person that you are talking to is the ultimate decision maker and what part of the sale process you are in. You will also need intuition to discover potential clients, and your intuition will improve if you stay curious and always ask discovery questions.

Confidence

Having confidence is essential to create trust and make the ask after your pitch and make the close. As an Executive Chauffeur, your confidence will be presented throughout your service. Your confidence will show when you are assertive about your driving skills, your knowledge of the route, your flawless service process, and your follow-up process. The best way to become confident is through preparation because proper preparation prevents poor performance and if you are prepared, you can be confident when asking for the business.

Character

Your character is the reflection of your reputation in the marketplace and your reputation is defined by how you follow through and deliver on your promises. Once your character is defined as dependable in your market, you, as the salesperson, will be able to generate new business through referrals.

Source: Patrick Bet-David, (Valuetainment), 08/10/2017, six qualities of great salespeople, YouTube.com

https://www.youtube.com/watch?v=ZuZBjpdvJQ8

Selling Skills

The following three different skills that a Chauffeur needs to master in order to maximize his/her income potential comes from a video posted on the YouTube channel named Valuetainment, presented by Patrick Bet-David. It explains the skills in detail so you can apply and become a successful salesperson.

I. Finder

A finder is someone that is great at

a. Finding new clients
b. Networking
c. Handing out business cards
d. Penetrating new markets
e. Getting through to the decision maker
f. Being approachable

I perceive this skill of finding new clients as introducing myself with the intent to leave the other person with information on what I have to offer. Here are a few examples of how I apply the skills of a FINDER.

I was assigned to drive a stretched GMC Sierra pickup truck limousine for a country style bachelorette party in Fort Worth, Texas. Once we got to the Stockyards and the clients went on to watch the rodeo, I stayed outside the limo with the doors opened with loud music playing while wearing my cowboy hat. The whole scene attracted people to check out the limo, and I ended up handing out over three hundred business cards that turned into many leads for the company.

Another example is when I was assigned to drive a brand-new Navigator during a Formula 1 event in NYC. I parked strategically close to the VIP venue entrance, where I could hand out cards and talk to many people of influence. I ended up meeting several personal assistants that became interested in my services for their employers.

Handing out cards and talking to people are not the only way to find potential sales, information is everywhere, so take advantage of it. Look for emails, phone numbers and social media profiles that can lead to direct contact. Look for future events where there will be a high concentration of people, make partnerships with companies, affiliates, and coworkers. Doing this will certainly lead to opportunities to seal your prospects.

II. Closer

A closer is someone that is great at

a. Being confident
b. Asking questions
c. Presenting
d. Reciting scripts
e. Answering frequently asked questions
f. Asking for the business

Closing deals take concentrated effort and intention. In order to succeed in closing deals, you have to be engaged in applying the qualities of a salesperson and follow the seven steps to a sale. Build your presentation based on what you offer. Stay curious so that you can ask the right questions and eliminate unnecessary concerns. Doing this will help you build a better presentation so that you can create trust more easily. Move the conversation forward while putting your prospect at ease with confidence. Be confident and audacious while asking for the business in ways that eliminate doubt.

It takes lots of practice and intention to be a CLOSER because it is the hardest skill to master since it involves knowing everything about your product or service. it requires you to know all the right answers to all the questions that your clients may have. It requires having the skills to present your product or service in a way that eliminates doubt and, most importantly, you must know when and how to ask for the business using the power of persuasion.

III. Developer

A developer is someone who is great at

a. Following up
b. Maintaining the relationship with the client
c. Addressing any concerns
d. Asking for referrals
e. Maintaining contact with the client
f. Providing customers satisfaction

Being a DEVELOPER is a skill that requires you to practice your social skills. Follow-ups and maintaining relationships is a full-time job because, if done right, it can generate revenue for a very long time. When you develop a relationship with your client, you get more chances to fix your mistakes and restore confidence in the relationship with your client. Clients are also more likely to refer to your product or service if they know that they can count on you because of that relationship.

These three skills are very hard to master and apply to your daily tasks, but if you can master these transferable skills, you will be able to maximize your opportunities and build a solid bulk of business that you can rely on.

Source: Patrick Bet-David, (Valuetainment), 03/28/2017, the three most important skills in sales, www.YouTube.com

https://www.youtube.com/watch?v=HZpE_TPxPT4

7 Steps to a Sale

As an Executive Chauffeur you will not always use the seven steps to a sale, but you need to know them in order to use them when appropriate.

Step 1: Prospect and qualify

Prospecting and Qualifying customers mean that you are actively searching for new clients and qualifying them to find out if they are willing and able to buy from you.

Step 2: Pre-approach

Pre-approach is simply doing your homework and finding out as much as possible about the potential client. All the Information found can be used to your advantage during the approach, presentation, and handling objections.

Step 3: Approach

Approaching involves an introduction, some small talk, some warmup questions and generally explaining who you are and what you represent. The goal of this process is to gain the trust of your prospect, so they become comfortable with you.

Step 4: Presentation

This is where all the research will make the difference. Your presentation and pitch should be tailored to each specific customer and by the time you got to this step you already have the person's trust and know what their needs are!

Step 5: Handle objections

After your sales presentation, your client usually has some hesitation in buying. This is where you address any concerns and solve any of their problems.

Step 6: Closing

Closing usually happens after handling objections. This is your time to ask for their business and solidify the transaction.

Step 7: Follow up

It is important to follow up with your client because, after you have established the relationship, you have to develop the relationship.

Source: https://www.lucidchart.com/blog/what-is-the-7-step-sales-process

Sale Script

Why should I choose your services?

- Sir/Ma'am, my services are not cheap, but they are not the most expensive
- My company is not the biggest, but it is large enough to fulfill all of your requests
- My company is not the smallest yet it is small enough where any issues that arise are resolved quickly and efficiently not by a computer but by one of our representatives, and if you need to, you can reach upper management just as fast as booking our services
- We do not focus on quantity; we rather focus on quality and that is why 80% of my business is composed of referrals and requests
- Now that you know more about my company, I ask you kindly to give me a chance to service you as one of our VIP clients

(Do not use all these examples on the pitch. Only use the ones that fit the conversation.)

Asking for Referrals

Sir/Ma'am, you have been using our services for a while. As you might know 80% of our business is composed of referrals and since we are slowly increasing our business, I would like to ask you if there is anyone that you could refer our business to in order to help us keep our business going?

Yes.

That is wonderful! How can I get in contact with that person? Or could I count on you to pass on my business card?

Great, thank you so much for your support! It means a great deal for me to know that I can count on you as you can count on me.

Thank you TEXT.

("Dear Mr./Ms. Smith, this is your Chauffeur, Alisson. It was a pleasure driving for you today. Please remember to refer our services to all of your friends and again, you can always request me as your Chauffeur. Enjoy the rest of your day!")

("Dear Mr./Ms. Smith, this is your Chauffeur, Alisson. I am just stopping to thank you for giving me the opportunity to drive for you today. I also want to thank you once again for your generosity! Have a wonderful day and I hope to see you again soon!")

Feel free to customize the text to your personality, but make sure you achieve the goal of encouraging repeat business.

Asking for Gratuity

Asking for gratuity can be uncomfortable, but there are proper ways to do it without being unprofessional.

The first example of how to do it is to automatically include a gratuity percentage on the bill. When this process is chosen, there must be full disclosure to the client at the time of booking.

The second example of how to ask for gratuity is to do it at the first contact with your client. *Example:* Hello Mr. Smith, I am your Chauffeur Alex and I just want to thank you in advance for giving me the opportunity to drive for you today and to thank you for your generosity up-front. Please let me know if there is any way that I can add value to your trip today!

This method is very efficient in injecting a thought of "I must tip" into your client's mind. But the one bad thing that this method does is that it decreases your referral rate since clients hate to feel obligated to spend more money. Clients will often treat the driver who uses this method as expandible and will change services rather quickly.

The third and most efficient example of how to ask for a tip is to insert a call to action into your business card. By this I mean add multiple payment QR codes to the back of your business card with the following phrase underneath "Tips are greatly appreciated, Thank you for your generosity!"

This method is the most efficient way to ask for a tip since the clients do not feel obligated to do so. This method also serves as a reminder to your clients in case they do not carry cash or if they leave without tipping.

This method will increase your tips because there is a call to action, it will increase your referral rate since you are passing on your business cards and it will increase your requests rates by staying in your customer's mind.

Please remember that tips are never mandatory and the only thing standing between you and a big tip is the quality of service that you provide.

Asking for Reviews

Asking for online reviews should be something that you, as the face of the company, should be asking every passenger for.

Here is an example of how to ask for an online review:

"Mr./Mrs. Smith, I hope this was a pleasant ride for you, it would mean the world to me if you could leave a positive online review of my services. Reviews help me reach my bonus and reviews are also a great source of new clients for me and the company! Thank you!"

"Hi Mr./Mrs. Smith, I'm just passing by to thank you for giving me the opportunity to drive for you today and to ask you for an online review so we can continue to get more amazing clients like yourself. Again, Thank you so much!"

Many companies already use this strategy, but have a much lower success rate since they are automated, and the customer does not feel any personal connection to the service. It is always more affective when the message reaches the customer via Text and from the person who had the most contact with the client.

People love helping others and if they can make a difference without any financial cost or significant investment of time, they will absolutely make an effort to help. Based on personal experience and in-house research, it is proven that there is an eighty to ninety percent success rate with such follow up text messages so, take advantage of this easy process to grow your customer base.

Social Media

In today's time, it is impossible to ignore social media since over 50% of the world's population uses it in some way. Social media has three types of users: Social Media platform owners, Businesses and Ordinary people. Social media is used by Platform owners to collect and sell data to businesses and governments, and to sell the space for businesses to use within the platform. Businesses use social media to collect consumer's data, network and to create relationships, to promote products and services, and to sell products and services. Social media is used by regular people to keep in touch with friends and family. They share moments, pictures, audio, documents, ideas, likes and dislikes.

Now that we know how social media is used and who uses it, we can apply our efforts into using Social Media Platforms to benefit our purpose of self-promoting and promoting our services.

Here are some tips on how you should use social media to promote yourself and your business.

1. **Create a social personal brand**
    a. Your personal brand should be authentic and always reflect who you really are and what you stand for. People or customers are only interested in real and consistent information because that is how you will create trust and convert interest into action.
    b. Present your core values and explain what they are.
    For example:
    AUTHENTIC you are real and honest about everything.

RELIABLE anyone can count on you if your word is given.
INVITING you are very personable and welcoming to any person.
RESOURCEFUL you are a problem solver and you will do anything to satisfy a request from a client.

c. Add value. All of your content should add value to people who consume it. Adding value can create a loyal following.
d. Work with multiple social media platforms, but you must be clear and consistent. Be consistent with your message, your platform appearance, and your service.
e. Avoid mixing your personal life with your professional life since it might create doubt or disinterest on your actual service potential.

2. **Any content that you create should be visually appealing, evoke emotions and call to action**

    a. Use visual communication, such as pictures that tell a story
    b. Tell the story in written format or video format
    c. Avoid controversial topics such as politics, sex, religion etc.
    d. Add value to the content and promote yourself or your business
    e. Call people to action by asking for them to like, share, subscribe, click the link below, call, email, etc.

All these tips can help you grow the number of followers you have because social media is an excellent way to use all the skills that you have learned in this training. You can use it to re-enforce lasting impressions, to create customer loyalty, and to generate new business.

TIPS & TRICKS

The following tips and tricks are suggestions of things that I have personally experienced and can help you through situations on the daily activities as an Executive Chauffeur.

- Get enough sleep! Working in the transportation industry can be very demanding of your time and too often we get caught doing time extensive jobs during times where your body should be resting in the form of sleep.
- Find out about the jobs when speaking to dispatchers and/or clients so that you can position yourself to be chosen for that specific job.
- When using tire shine, always wipe off the excess to keep it from splattering on the side of the vehicle when in motion.
- Get a solid color napkin or a napkin with your logo, fold it diagonally forming a triangle, wrap it around the premium bottle of water and place it in the cup holder. Doing this shows that you care and adds a feeling of luxury to your service. Do Not use white napkins or cheap fast-food napkins as it is available everywhere and not exclusive.
- Use a microfiber cloth to wipe the interior of your vehicle, it is much easier to remove handprints and fingerprints from shiny surfaces.
- When texting your client, only add Ms. or Mr. in front of their name if you know who they are to avoid any gender confusion.
- Say your clients name at least three times during the ride so that they feel important and recognized. Always address them as Ms. or Mr.
- When your passenger is entering or exiting the vehicle, face the rear of the vehicle and open the door with the hand that is closest to the vehicle, as the passenger enters the vehicle you should move be-

hind them to protect their back and see if they are completely inside before you shut the door. When your passenger is getting out, do the opposite procedure, stepping away from the client and behind the door to give them space.

- When opening and closing doors, make sure to prioritize opening the door for elderly first, then for women and children second, and lastly for men.
- When picking up a client at a public location such as an airport; make sure that you are picking up the right passenger. On an occasion where I was at the airport holding a name sign, a random person pretended to be my assigned client and informed that we had to change the drop off address. Unfortunately, I fell for this trap that time and ended up driving for this person for free while my real passenger was still at the airport waiting for me. People will pose as someone else to get a free ride, so do your research and be aware of who you are picking up.
- When your client is a celebrity, pay special attention when they are getting in and out of the vehicle. Help protect them from fans and paparazzi until they are safe and locked inside the vehicle.
- When your client is of high profile and is accompanied by security, you should always follow the security guard's lead and lock the doors when the client is inside it.
- When your client is wearing a skirt, protect their dignity by blocking the view of outsiders while the client is getting in and out of the vehicle. Use your body with your back facing the client or an opened umbrella.

- When driving for women and elderly clients; always offer your forearm for support when exiting the vehicle.
- When a client is talking to another passenger or on the phone about something personal and they try to include you, just pause for a second and say, " excuse me, I can't hear you very well, are you speaking to me?" Often, they will say it was nothing and keep you out of it. If they do continue, just do not be intrusive.
- When communicating with a booker from abroad, ALWAYS, tell them that they can always request you as a Chauffeur.
- When you know that you will be transporting children 12 years old or younger, be prepared to make an animal balloon, because it might keep them entertained during the ride.
- When you know that you will be transporting any children 12 years old or younger, make an animal balloon for them and give to them so they can be entertained during the ride.
- If your client requests a child car seat, you should let them install it for liability purposes. If they ask for an installed child car seat; always make sure that they check to see if it is properly installed before the child sits down on it.
- Make an effort to learn how to greet people in different languages. This comes in handy when driving for foreigners and it is also a great conversation starter.

- Listen to your clients' conversations, they often mention things they like and do not like. This information can be useful to adjust for a better service next time you are requested to drive the same client.
- Make sure to have good restaurants to suggest to your clients in case they ask you for recommendation.
- Make sure you know the tourist attractions available in the area in case your client asks for a recommendation.
- Consider bringing your own healthy meals as it will keep you from spending on food and keep you away from fast food and overeating because you are limited to what you have already packed. Just remember not to eat in the car but, if you do, just make sure to clean up after yourself and get rid of food odors.
- When riding in a convoy, make sure to stay coordinated with the other drivers and security detail.
- If you carry a firearm, make sure it is concealed. You never know if the client or passenger is pro-gun or against the second amendment.
- If you carry a firearm, make sure that you know how to safely operate your firearm in order to prevent any accidents. Keep your firearm holstered at all times and do not unholster it just to show someone.

Follow the four rules of firearm safety!

1. ALWAYS KEEP YOUR FIREARM POINTED IN A SAFE DIRECTION.
2. TREAT ALL FIREARMS AS IF THEY WERE LOADED.

3. KEEP YOUR TRIGGER FINGER OUTSIDE THE GUARD AND OFF OF THE TRIGGER UNTIL YOU ARE READY TO FIRE.
4. BE CERTAIN OF YOUR TARGET, YOUR LINE OF FIRE, AND WHAT LIES BEYOND YOUR TARGET.

   It is encouraged that you take a firearm safety course if you intend to carry a firearm.

   P.S. I am not a firearm safety instructor, so you must do your due diligence!

- Never have your phone synced to the vehicle while your client is onboard because you never know when you will receive an unexpected call.
- Research your client on the web and find out everything you can about your client so that you can use that information to your advantage.
- Always keep at least $20 in change in case you need it. Your client will often give you a tip and in many instances, they will need change, sometimes you will need to pay tolls that require cash and sometimes have to pay for parking that only accept cash.
- If your client is sleeping in the vehicle when you arrive at the destination, turn the radio off and ask them a question that is relevant to the end of their ride. For example:

Sir/Ma'am, are you checking your bag outside or inside?

Sir/Ma'am, will you need the vehicle for later today?

Sir/Ma'am, do you need help with your luggage? Etc.

They normally wake up when someone calls their name.

- Keep a MULTI-TOOL set in your Chauffeur bag in case you need any tools for basic fixes.
- Keep an electric jump cable in your vehicle should your battery die.
- Learn how to organize luggage in the trunk of your vehicle so that you can do it in a safe and efficient way. Always place the luggage in a way that it will not move forward if you must break suddenly.
- Learn about airport travel procedures in advance so that you and your clients are ready.

Airport procedures may include:

1. Proper pick up and drop off locations.
2. Outside and Inside check in locations.
3. Proper check in times for domestic flights (at least 1 hour before boarding time)
4. Proper check in times for international flights (three hours before boarding time)
5. Pre-check benefits if the clients are not checking luggage.
6. Global Entry Pass clients will go through airport security much faster that those without Global Entry Pass.
7. If there is a greeter, you must coordinate a meetup location beforehand.

8. If you are meeting the client inside the terminal, you must know where the closest parking area is in order to expedite getting to the vehicle.
9. When servicing a client at a private FBO, you must know the aircraft's tail number and the FBO safety procedures.

- It is unlikely but it can happen that you get a rowdy, unstable or unreasonable passenger in your vehicle so, I encourage you to learn how to deescalate situations in order to keep the standards of service and safety.
- If you are driving a stretched limousine, keep a 2ft by 3ft red rug in the trunk so that you can welcome your clients with a red carpet. "You only need to lay it out for the client on the first time that they are entering the vehicle".
- If you are driving a party bus or a party van, set boundaries at the beginning of the service so that you do not encounter undesired behavior from the passengers.

14

DO NOT DO!

The following are suggestions of things not to do while on the job. These are things that I have personally experienced and can help you navigate through situations on the daily activities as an Executive Chauffeur.

- NEVER argue with a paying customer. You will never win because customers are always right, even if they are wrong!
- Do not chew gum.
- Do not smoke in the vehicle.
- Do not eat in the vehicle.
- Do not have big key chains that will make rattling noises during the drive.
- Do not ask personal questions of your clients.
- Do not get involved in controversial conversations.
- Do not speed.
- Do not drive recklessly.
- Do not arrive late.
- Do not panic when a problem arises.
- Do not oversell.
- Do not text and drive.
- Do not contact your client if it is not for something related to their ride.
- Do not swear in front of clients.
- Do not talk about confidential information from clients to other clients.
- Do not mention clients' names to other clients.
- Do not slouch.
- Do not interrupt your client's conversation.
- Do not invade the client's personal space.

- Do not make your clients wait.
- Do not make excuses.
- Do not sexually harass your client.
- Do not make inappropriate comments to your client.
- Do not let your client carry their own luggage unless they want to.
- Do not leave your vehicle opened.
- Do not throw garbage out of the window.
- Do not change your vehicle's sound tone settings.
- NEVER accept or allow any illegal activity in the vehicle.
- NEVER consume alcoholic beverages while on the job.
- NEVER pose or promise to be a personal security guard. Unless you have credentials, and you are being paid to do so.
- Do not break the law in order to satisfy client's requests.
- Do not break the law in order to create convenience.

15

PANDEMIC

The job of an Executive Chauffeur was hard enough before the pandemic, but COVID-19 changed people's perspectives about the necessity to travel, imposed barriers in the way people travel and communicate, and forced adaptation; making it even harder for Chauffeurs to succeed. Due to restricted travel during the height of the 2020 pandemic, people had time to think about their situations and optimize their necessity to commute or travel on the regular basis. Because of this change in behavior, the transportation industry took a massive economic hit, leaving thousands of companies without revenue, therefore, leaving thousands of people unemployed. The situation imposed those businesses to change and adapt to the new norms in order to be successful.

One of the biggest changes that people encountered is the necessity of wearing masks. People are naturally afraid of putting themselves at risk, so wearing a mask became a necessity. Masks are great for preventing the spread of illnesses, but it created some big challenges for Chauffeurs.

The first challenge that masks created is that it changed first impressions, you were judged on if you were wearing a mask; if you were wearing it properly, and what kind of mask you were wearing.

The second challenge that masks created is that it is much harder to recognize people and read facial expressions, forcing Chauffeurs to be more expressive with their eyes and volume of voice.

The third challenge that masks have presented is that masks have muffled our voices, so communication has naturally decreased since people would rather stay in silence than to put in the effort to increase their tone or volume of voice. Not only that but, people also tend to stay in silence in order to decrease the amount of gases or particulate matter exhaled when talking.

The fourth challenge that masks have presented is that masks have covered our nose so that we cannot properly detect certain smells making it harder to compliment someone on their perfume, determine if the vehicle is thoroughly clean and odorless or if the vehicle has any problems such as the smell of leaking fuel, oil or burned smell of overheated breaks.

Another challenge that masks present is for drivers who wear glasses, not only is it uncomfortable, but it also fogs up the glasses, creating a hazardous situation by obstructing the view of the driver.

Another change that companies and Chauffeurs had to make is that Chauffeurs also had to make adaptations to their vehicle, such as adding a clear shield that separates the clients from the Chauffeur. This has become an added barrier to communication and vehicle operation. It is much harder to hear and understand what the passengers are saying because of the sound barrier. It is also harder to interpret facial expressions and read body language because of glare or reflections made by the plastic partitions. When it comes to operating the vehicle, the same problems apply. The plastic partitions create a sound barrier from anything coming from behind and create glare or reflections that distract you from seeing potential hazards on the sides and behind the vehicle.

Not only masks and clear partitions in the vehicle created new procedures, but differentiated sanitation also added to the new norms of any transportation business. The sanitation process of the vehicle has changed dramatically because of COVID-19. Chauffeurs or companies are forced to invest in disinfectants, harsh chemicals, and machinery in order to operate safely. Chauffeurs now must use harsh chemicals to sanitize the interior of the vehicle by using specialized fog machines or sprays before any client enters the vehicle. Chauffeurs also must wipe down high touch areas with disinfectants and improve air quality in the vehicle by not using recirculated air functions in the vehicle and drive with windows open.

Before COVID-19 appeared, Chauffeurs were easily noticed by the quality and variety of amenities that were made available to the clients. After COVID-19 became part of our lives, Chauffeurs were forced to eliminate all amenities in the vehicle. The purpose of eliminating amenities in the vehicle was to decrease the amount of surface area and high touch areas in the vehicle. Amenities that are considered high touch areas would be magazines, phone chargers, tissue boxes, candy jars, pens, papers, water bottles etc.... Chauffeurs are now limited to hand sanitizer, disposable gloves, and spare masks. Other high touch areas in the vehicle would be handles, levers, seat belts, holders, knobs, etc. This restriction has created a barrier to differentiation, therefore decreasing the success rate of any effort to creating lasting positive impressions.

Thankfully, the pandemic is no longer a severe issue, and we are now back to living normal lives. Unfortunately, today, after the pandemic, masks and sanitation procedures still make people judge each other because if someone is still afraid of the virus and still wears a mask, that person might be judged by others who might think that they are carrying the virus because they are wearing a mask. None the less, the 2020 pandemic has not only opened our eyes to how fragile humans and businesses are, but it has also revealed how resilient and resourceful humans can be.

This period in time has also forced people to practice solving problems and overcoming challenges by applying the following principles: Identifying the problem, evaluating the problem, strategizing the process, implementing the resources and overcoming the problem. Obstacles and setbacks will always be present in our lives, so we must do our best to optimize opportunities during these hard times. Remember that the results will always reflect the amount of effort you put in!

CONCLUSION

After going through all the information in this book, we now understand everything that all the paying customer's wants and needs and by doing so we can apply all the principles needed to fulfill those wants and needs. Remember that all the topics discussed in this book are transferable skills and can be adapted and applied to any career path you chose. We have also gathered enough information to have a new definition of a true Chauffeur.

The dictionary defines a Chauffeur as a person employed to drive a private or rented automobile for a certain amount of time to and from certain locations.

For most of your clients a Chauffeur is a high-end vehicle driver with a suit on, but an Executive Chauffeur is a stylish driver who can get them from point A to point B on a timely fashion with the highest level of luxury and class while fulfilling all requests and expectations; you are essentially a butler on wheels.

On the other hand, to Limousine companies and work colleagues an Executive Chauffeur is a person who is, very hygienic, presentable, well structured, approachable, perfectionist, great communicator, highly adaptive, service oriented, proactive, great driver, secret keeper, salesman and friend.

Most importantly, an Executive Chauffeur is a transformer of excellent service into revenue by differentiating him or herself and communicating his or her unique value.

Now that you are equipped with all the knowledge necessary to become an Executive Chauffeur, the real work begins!

As Patrick Bet David always says, "You must out work, out improve, out strategize, and out last your competitors and your enemies so that you can one day become the best in the industry." And as Thomas Elsworth always says, "I hope I left you better than when I found you!"

Stay curious and apply all the knowledge that you have just gained!

Now that you have finished reading the book, your next step is to leave an honest review on amazon.com. Your review is very important to me as it will help me reach more readers, and change more people's lives for the better!

Thank you for your support!

Executive Chauffeur Alisson T. Guimaraes

ACKNOWLEDGMENTS

First and foremost, I thank God for giving me the willingness to try something new. Writing was never a big focus of mine, but someway and somehow this piece came together with one personal experience at a time that led to a thought, then led to notes on paper, then turned into cohesive, useful information.

To my lovely wife Monique, for being part of my life and accepting me for who I am. For supporting me and trusting me as her partner and providing me with the thing I value most: FAMILY.

To my precious daughters Elena and Rebecca, who will grow into honorable women just like their mother.

To my parents Marly and Joao Carlos, for loving me unconditionally and supporting me in the bad times and the good times.

To my brother Halder, a principled, loving man who has in many ways influenced me into becoming the man I am today!

To my Grandmother Nair, who has shown me that positivity and faith are the key to overcoming any problem in life, regardless of its severity.

Lastly, I dedicate this piece to YOU, the reader, and I hope that the information in this book can influence you into becoming a successful professional in whatever field you work in.

ABOUT THE AUTHOR

Alisson Guimaraes is an Executive Chauffeur with a goal of elevating the standards of professionalism. With no formal training available when he began his career, Alisson relied on detailed observations and advice from fellow drivers and customers. Recognizing the need for comprehensive guidance, he authored "The Ultimate Chauffeur" as a course-like resource for any individual wanting to elevate their skills in the area of professionalism. His goal is to help unqualified individuals become skilled professionals, improving their lives and careers in every way possible.

He is originally from Brazil. Educated In three different cultures, three different languages and an expert in adaptation.

He is a graduate from IONA College an AACSB accredited university, with a Bachelors degree in International Business Administration from The Hagan School of Business and he is also a graduate from the State University of New York at Westchester Community College with a degree in Arts and Science.

In over twenty years of hospitality service, sales, administration and management, Alisson has learned to adjust to many personalities and react to uncountable circumstances.

All his jobs to date have had some type of transportation and client service involved; therefore, exposing him to the skills needed to execute the chauffeuring service.

Alisson lives in Dallas, Texas with his wife and daughters.

CONTACT ALISSON

Follow **The Ultimate Chauffeur** on social media.

Handle: **@theultimatechauffeur**

For online training and certification visit the website:

WWW.ULTIMATECHAUFFEUR.COM

For special offers, consulting or speaking services

e-mail:

ALISSON@ULTIMATECHAUFFEUR.COM

Printed in Great Britain
by Amazon

62139854R00097